Solo Coastal Sailing

A how-to book for the sailor who seeks solitude or who can't find suitable crew

© 2017 by **Colin Stroud**

First edition January 26, 2015
Updated February 17, 2017

I can never remember a time when I was not fascinated by boats and the water. By the time I was thirteen I began teaching myself to sail by hiring a 3m clinker sailing dinghy on the local park lake. Without any friends or relatives interested in sailing who could give me advice, and without any help from the lake attendant, interested only in taking the money, trial and error had to be my teacher. And a wonderful teacher it was. That "lake" was no more than 200m across, so I had to learn very quickly how to keep off the lee shore.

By the age of twenty I had progressed to both helming and crewing in high speed trapeze dinghies. I did slow down a bit to build a motor yacht in order to explore the English east coast rivers, but sailing was my first love and I moved back to sailing in cruising yachts.

In the last four decades I have sailed thousands of miles in all kinds of weather, in many sea conditions and in a range of boats. I've explored coasts, rivers and estuaries, sailed in company and alone, competed in regattas, and even won some prizes. And almost all of it has been single-handed.

I currently sail a "Heard 23, Falmouth Working Boat". This heavy displacement, long keel, gaff cutter is proving to be an ideal boat for solo coastal sailing. Whatever boat you select, you can have the same joy I experience when the sounds of the wind and the sea are my only companions. Single-handed coastal sailing is truly rewarding.

I have included some more about me at the very end of this eBook.

Colin Stroud

Figure 1 – a small wooden clinker gunter-rigged dinghy of the
type first sailed solo by the author over 40 years ago

TRIBUTE

To Sharon, my wife and occasional sailing partner.

and

to the following friends for their contributions, assistance and moral support:-

Bernard Patrick
Mike McCarthy
Mary-Alice and Richard Jafolla
Rob Farrell

and to

Dynamic Consultants (dynco.co.uk)
For helping me to build my own website.
(Search for "solocoastalsailing")

CONTENTS

Solo Coastal Sailing

INTRODUCTION

Every sailor has his or her own goal—sailing an ocean, crossing the English Channel or making a short passage up the coast to the next safe harbour. Each requires a different solution, each requires different techniques. Many sailors have written books about their voyages and experiences, but those writing about single-handed sailing have mostly been the ocean crossers. They focus on sustainability in terms of food, water and fuel, and on managing storms when there is no opportunity for running to a safe haven. And books about shorter excursions? They tend to focus more on the experience, places and how to navigate there, rather than any specific advice on managing the boat alone.

Figure 1 – it's all down to you – no crew to worry about

This book is for the sailor with more modest goals, probably the majority of us. We may dream of selling up and setting off on grand voyages around the world visiting other countries, but in reality most yachtsmen and yachtswomen get all the enjoyment they need from a 30 mile trip to a favourite harbour in the next county. Doing this safely with no one to help you does require some additional skills. No one set of skills will work for everyone and there is no substitute for practicing in small stages, but in the following pages I will be passing on to you what has worked for me.

Figure 2 – sailing alone can be fun

If, after reading all the theory, the thought of making that first solo passage is still too daunting, then at first take along an experienced friend. But he or she should be under strict instructions to let you do all the work. (This is the type of crew that are easier to find!)

Why Single-handed?

One of the hardest decisions you make when sailing is abandoning a voyage due to worsening weather when the boat and crew are ready to sail. You fight the temptation to ignore the forecasters, or assume they are being overly cautious, and take a chance for the sake of not disappointing your team. Having your shipmates standing by expecting an enjoyable day out, after weeks of expectation and planning, puts you under an extreme amount of pressure to continue with the trip.

Figure 3 – you can set off any time it suits you

How much easier if you were alone. You jump aboard, pick up a good book and stay in port until the wind decreases, all without having a guilty conscience.

Or it could be you have problems finding crew when you want to go sailing. If having others aboard is more about having extra hands and eyes to help run the ship, rather than the need for comradeship, then learning how to sail single-handed will enable you to go out more often, particularly at a time to suit you.

Figure 4 – sailing alone can be relaxing

A Rewarding Experience

Sailing a yacht on your own can be a very rewarding experience. By exchanging crew for some additional yacht-management skills you can be far more relaxed than with other people aboard and having to worry about their safety and be constantly alert to their moods, movements and wishes.

Of course there are times when having partner, family and friends with you will make a memorable voyage. I love sailing with my wife, but she does not share the same degree of passion and becomes frightened in less than ideal conditions. As a result I tend to get edgy and nervous.

Sharing experiences can make it twice as much fun, true, but for me the real joy is the utter relaxation of sailing alone.

*"To young men contemplating a voyage
I would say go"*

Joshua Slocum, the first person to sail single-handed around the world, between 1895 and 1898.

WHICH BOAT IS BEST

There is no one particular type of boat most suitable for the lone sailor. I am assuming you would not be planning to set off on your own without already having some hands-on sailing experience with crew, so probably the best boat of all will be the one you already have. It takes at least a season (and probably three) to really understand the characteristics of a boat in a range of weather and sea conditions, so why not short cut this and work with what you've got and already know?

If you are between boats or unsatisfied with the one you have, then you have more opportunity to build single-handing ability into your criteria for the next one.

How do you choose?

So much about the choice of boat is a matter of individual taste and experience and the usual advice is to start by deciding on the type of sea area in which you will sail. But (if you believe what the manufacturers tell you) that leads you into lists of almost every boat there is. All boats above 2.5m long built or sold in the European Union (EU) since June 16, 1998, have to meet the essential safety requirements set down in the European Union Recreational Craft Directive (RCD) 2003/44/EC, which dictates these categories for them --

RCD Category A - Ocean: Designed for extended voyages where conditions may exceed wind force 8 (Beaufort scale) and significant wave heights of 4m and above but excluding abnormal conditions, and vessels largely self-sufficient.

RCD Category B - Offshore: Designed for offshore voyages where conditions up to and including wind force 8 and significant wave heights up to and including 4m may be experienced.

Figure 5 – typical examples of boats that comply with the four RCD categories

RCD Category C - Inshore: Designed for voyages in coastal waters, large bays, estuaries, lakes and rivers where conditions up to and including wind force 6 and significant wave heights up to and including 2m may be experienced.

RCD Category D - Sheltered: Designed for voyages on sheltered coastal waters, small bays, small lakes, rivers and canals where conditions up to and including wind force 4 and significant wave heights up to and including 0.3m may be experienced, with occasional waves of 0.5m maximum height, for example from passing vessels.

Because they are intended to improve safety as well as create unified standards throughout the EU, these RCD categories should not be ignored. Using a boat in waters more exposed than its certification may be perfectly safe in the right hands, but it may make your insurance void should you need to make a claim.

A basic starting point

Consideration of the above categories can still leave you with a wide range of options, so I believe a more fundamental starting point is to decide on one of these three categories:-

- Open boats.
- Boats with a small cabin.
- Boats with a cabin in which you can stand up.

Open boats

Many epic voyages have been made in open boats. Margaret and Frank Dye are both famous for extended passages, both together and alone, in a 5m Wayfarer dingy. With an open boat you can spend a night aboard in harbour under a fabric cover or even in a tent ashore. Contact the UK based Dinghy Cruising Association or check out their website at http://dinghycruising.org.uk/ for lots of advice. These boats tend to be small, however, and so are mostly limited to the number of people on board. This makes them obvious choices for single-handers, provided their limitations in open waters are recognised.

You do not have to be the brave and intrepid explorer type to single-hand an open boat. If you pick the right cruising ground with lots of sheltered water and interconnecting creaks and rivers, you can remain safe and satisfied.

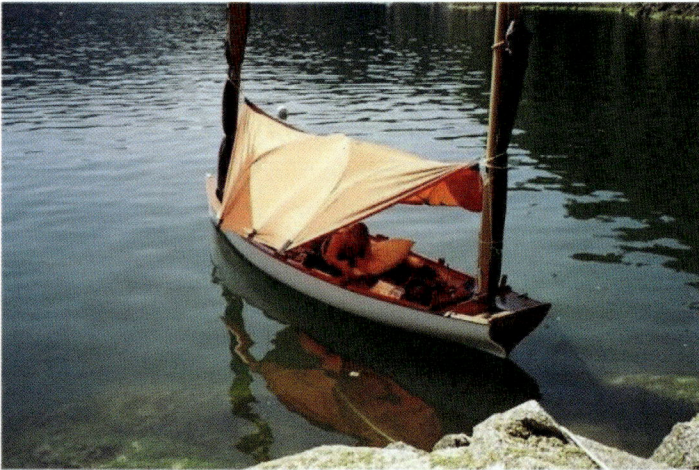

Figure 6 – space for one - cruising in an open boat

Coastal passages require much more careful planning and studying of weather forecasts, but one of the advantages of an open boat is that if the weather worsens and you cannot sail back from a haven, telephoning a friend to drive your car and trailer to fetch you can save the day -- assuming you had the foresight to leave a spare car key with someone!

These smaller craft can also be less reliant on mechanical propulsion and are easily propelled by a good pair of oars when the wind dies or when needing to come alongside the slipway.

Boats with a small cabin

Unlike an open boat with temporary accommodation, these have obvious benefits in terms of convenient and dry accommodation and storage. Although lacking in headroom, they can make an ideal single-handed boat for sheltered as well as coastal sailing. The sales brochures always quote umpteen berths, but I believe they must be assuming all crew bring no extra clothes, waterproofs, boots or bedding because there is usually nowhere to store it all once all the essential boat equipment is on board. Ideal for one person.

Figure 7 – a small yacht with sitting headroom in the cabin

Craft of this type, usually less than 7m long, are usually easy to sail in terms of strength to handle the gear, although their diminutive size and light weight make them less comfortable on lumpy water. Yet, they usually have shallow draft and/or a lifting keel, which means you can often take a short-cut across the shallows to reach a sheltered anchorage that a larger boat would struggle to reach. It's all a compromise.

Boats with a cabin in which you can stand up

The human frame comes in many shapes and sizes, so the yacht designer needs to account for a significant proportion of this spectrum so as not to exclude too many potential buyers. To accommodate 95 percent of the adult UK male population a cabin would need 1.86m of headroom.

Figure 8 – typical yacht with standing headroom in the cabin

The standing headroom factor limits the minimum size of the boat, which is unlikely to be less that 7m and probably more than 8m long unless, of course you are lucky enough to be at or below average height. If you want shallow draft as well as standing headroom then, unless you can live with an excessively high superstructure whose windage will be disproportionately large and therefore affect the sailing performance, you will have to go for an even longer craft in order not to have to stoop.

Three important considerations

In addition to choosing from the above three groupings, I believe three important considerations relevant to sailing on your own should be:-

- Stability
- Upper size limit
- Type of rig (covered in chapter 2)

Stability

Movable human ballast can be very handy when it comes to counteracting the pressure of wind on sails, but is in short supply on the single-handed yacht. A tippy yacht that needs three people on the rail to counteract the effects of a force-4 breeze will probably be too much of a handful for one person.

The challenge is to find the best compromise between sail area and righting moment for your particular needs. Of course, you can set smaller sails or reef sooner as the wind increases, yet it may be less stressful if the boat can stand up to a wider spread of wind strengths. But here is that compromise again -- there may be a trade-off against speed. The ballast / displacement ratio is a measure of the stability of a boat's hull. Basically it describes how well a boat will stand up to its sails and is often quoted in magazine reviews and sometimes by manufacturers. This ratio may not help in the first stages of narrowing your choice of boats but becomes very useful when comparing those in a short-list.

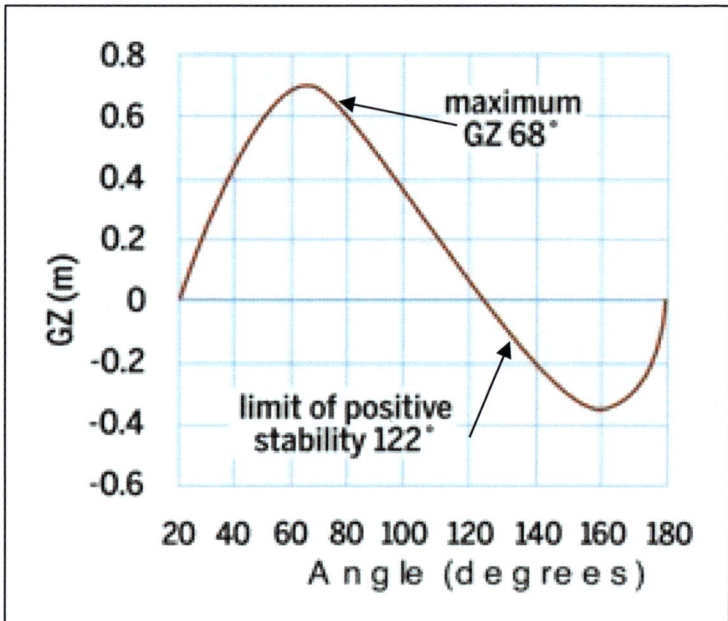

Figure 9 – a typical yacht stability curve showing the "Limit of Positive Stability", also known as the "Angle of Vanishing Stability"

Many boat specifications now include stability curves that indicate the "limit of positive stability", also called the Angle of Vanishing Stability (AVS), which is the angle of heel beyond which the hull will not self-right. This can be misleading, as a hull can be very stable and have a comfortable motion in a seaway yet still be liable to capsize beyond, say, 90 degrees of heel.

Understanding the GZ Curve

The transverse horizontal distance between the Centre of Gravity and Centre of Buoyancy is known as the righting arm (GZ). With heel angle increasing from left to right and the righting arm plotted vertically, the GZ curve will tell you several things about a boat's stability.

The angle of the upward leg of the curve indicates the initial stiffness of the boat. A shallow angle would indicate, for example, that the boat is initially tender; a steep angle points to a boat that has high initial stability. The top of the curve marks the maximum righting arm; after this point is passed the boat will become progressively less stable as GZ decreases. The intersection of the upper portion of the curve with the zero-GZ line marks the LPS (Limit of Positive Stability), also called the AVS (Angle of Vanishing Stability). Below the line to the right of the LPS is the negative area, which indicates how stable the boat will be when inverted.

Just as with the positive portion of the curve, a steep angle to the negative curve as it approaches 180 degrees of heel indicates a boat that is initially stable--but upside down. A shallow angle is desirable and indicates a boat with "poor" inverted stability. The lowest point of the curve indicates the maximum inverted moment, and the negative area inside the curve is a measure of the wave energy that would be required to right the boat. The ideal is a shallow curve with a maximum negative GZ that's less than 50 percent of the maximum positive GZ, with a negative area less than one-fifth that of the positive area. Most modern production boats will have LPS angles of between 100 and 140 degrees.

The International Standard dealing with the stability of mono-hull ballasted sailing yachts, ISO 12217-2, uses a "stability index", or STIX, for quantifying stability. STIX is calculated from the physical characteristics of each boat and is a number generally in the range 5 to 50. A higher value suggests greater stability. The STIX value, along with the AVS, is used to place the boat into one of the four RCD categories mentioned earlier.

However, these categories, indexes and values do not tell you how comfortable the boat's motion will be in a rough sea. Nor do they tell you how seaworthy or safe they will be. They tell you only how stable they are designed to be.

The comfort factor

The aspect probably most important to the lone sailor is a boat's "comfort factor". Consider being tossed about like a cork versus a levitation-like ride where the hull appears oblivious to the waves approaching from all angles. With no crew to share the workload, too much pitching and rolling can be very tiring, so a stable hull has huge advantages for the solo sailor.

Ted Brewer, a lifelong sailor and yacht designer with over 260 designs to his credit and author of "Understanding Boat Design", now in its fourth edition, developed an empirical measure of comfort. He called it the "Comfort Ratio" and his measure of motion comfort which has been widely accepted, provides a reasonable comparison between yachts.

The Ted Brewer Comfort Ratio (CR) formula is:
$$D / (0.65 \times (0.7\ LWL + 0.3\ LOA) \times B^{1.333})$$

Where:
D = Displacement in pounds
LWL = Length of Water Line in feet
LOA = Length Over All of the hull in feet
B = maximum Beam in feet

Large CR numbers indicate a smoother, more comfortable motion in a sea-way. The equation favours heavy boats with lots of overhang and a narrow beam. These are all factors that slow down a boat's response in violent conditions, which contribute greatly in reducing crew fatigue.

This design philosophy is contrary to many modern racer/cruiser yachts which are often designed for speed in calm waters or for accommodation volume. A ratio of 29 is the low end of the comfort range. A value of 30 to 40 is recommended for a cruising boat. Racing designs are typically less than 30, and a full keel Colin Archer design could be as high as 55. My current 23 foot Falmouth Working Boat has a CR of just over 40.

"Natural roll period"
Another measure of comfort is the "Natural Roll Period", where Roll Period (T) =
$$2*PI*((D^{1.744}/35.5)/(82.43*LWL*(.82*B)^3))^{.5}$$

The roll period is based on the moment of inertia, waterline length, and beam. The moment of inertia is very sensitive to the distance items are from the CG (centre of gravity). A heavy rig can greatly change the roll characteristic, with little impact on displacement.

Rather than using complex formulae, the easiest way of determining a yacht's roll rate is to simply grab a shroud and push / pull until the boat is rocking over a few degrees. Then measure the time it takes for ten full cycles, and divide by 10.

The general rule of thumb is that boats with periods less than 4 seconds are stiff and periods greater than 8 seconds are tender, but short periods can be very uncomfortable with a jerky motion. Too long may mean there is not enough initial stability. So once again, this does not tell you what is right or wrong, just another way of using quantitative data to compare yachts on your list.

Upper size limit

In short, there isn't one. But, there is always a "but". The limiting factor will always be your own strength. The famous 1960's yacht designer, Kim Holman, considered a waterline length of 7.3m a minimum for good hull speed and the maximum for ease of handling.

If you are planning to cross oceans or circle the globe, then ease of entering port or marina will be low on your wants list. But the average single-handed yachtsperson enters harbour each day. Berthing or mooring a boat over 10m can be very challenging, not to mention handling the large sails that are necessary. With no one to help, you will either need to invest in some labour saving devices or limit the size and effort required by choosing a boat within your ability.

Figure 10 – the "Twister" design by Kim Holman

There are some impressive sheet and halyard winches in the chandlers that will make light work of sail handling on a 20m boat, but at a considerable financial cost. Similarly, powered anchor windlasses and bow thrusters can reduce the effort needed, but all these devices bring their own problems of complexity and reliability. If any one of these devices were to fail, could you still safely manage the boat back to harbour on your own?

The type of sailing rig can influence your boat size. Take the spritsails of a Thames sailing barge or the junk rig from the Far East -- both are renowned for their ease of handling but they each have limitations and cannot be simply adapted to an existing mast or hull. The traditional gaff rig, used extensively for working craft before the internal combustion engine, evolved to allow maximum efficiency with minimal effort to enable a greater focus on the work in hand, whether that be dredging for shellfish or delivering a ship's pilot.

Figure 11 – the traditional working boat rig evolved as one that was easy to handle with limited crew

Here there is also a conflict with the earlier consideration of stability. A higher ballast ratio makes for a stable platform in a seaway, but this results in a heavier boat to handle in the confines of a marina when the wind is blowing hard. Yes, it will have higher inertia so manoeuvring will be more predictable with no sudden movements in a sudden gust of wind, but it will be more difficult to stop and do more damage to anything it hits. Once again, it's all a case of compromise and trade-off.

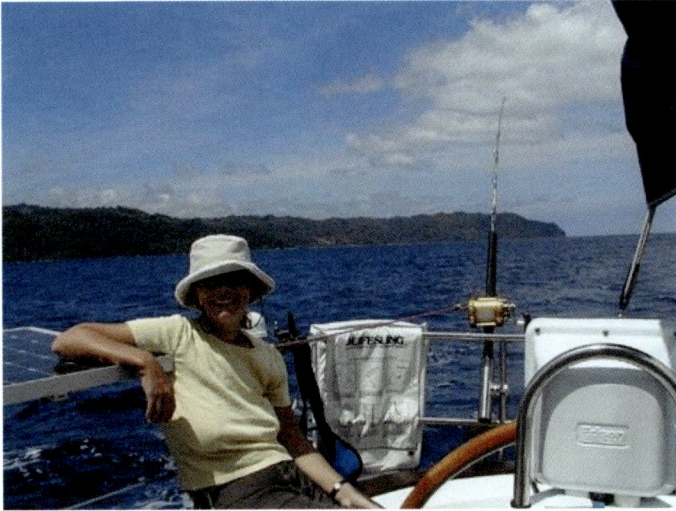

Figure 12 – the cockpit should be comfortable – you will be
spending a lot of time in it

Other considerations when choosing a boat

A comfortable cockpit is highly desirable. You'll be spending
a lot of time in it. Make sure there are lots of stowage nooks
in the cockpit or just inside the companionway, as it gets to
be a pain to run down into the cabin for binoculars, torch,
coffee, snacks, etc. When single-handing, there's no one
below to hand things up or take things down for you.

Most other considerations are not specific to the single-
handed yacht but there are, of course, many personal
preferences such as rear or centre cockpit, draft or keel
type. The latter two are dependant on the area you intend to
sail: shallow or deep, hard or soft bottom.

At the end of the day, most factors come down to personal experience. There is no substitute for getting out on the water in as many types of boat as you can in order to increase your knowledge and highlight what does and does not appeal to you.

"The only way to get a good crew is to marry one"

Eric Hiscock who, together with his wife Susan, were the first couple to sail two circumnavigations, between 1952 and 1968.

TYPE OF RIG

Every experienced solo sailor will have his or her own preference for a particular configuration of sails and masts. Certainly a wide variety of rigs can be managed single-handed. A better question is: What characteristics of a boat and rig make it easier to single-hand?

Good balance and a well-mannered helm are at the top of the list. I don't care what kind of rig you have, if you have to wrestle the helm when things get rough it is difficult to do much else. You can buy an expensive autopilot to do the wrestling, but it will work better and use less energy (battery watts) if the boat has a good helm.

The ideal single-hander balances well enough so the helm can be left alone, locked, lashed or pegged to keep on course long enough for you to reef or use the heads. The more traditional, low aspect ratio rigs are easier to trim to balance the helm.

The twin headsails of a cutter and the mizzen sail of a ketch or yawl provide more scope, especially when matched to a long keel that will help to keep you heading in a straight line. The tall narrow Bermudian rig on a flat bottomed deep fin keeled hull may be more demanding to sail in a blow, but you will usually get to a safe haven in half the time. However, the trade-off against that greater speed will be the lack of holding a track when you stop controlling the helm. Steering a modern lightweight sailboat can be a full time job.

Figure 13 – sail area spread fore and aft, as in a gaff yawl, provides more scope for a balanced helm

If trimming the sails does not improve balance you can alter the balance of a rig by physically moving the centre of effort fore or aft to help reduce the load on the helm. For example, adjusting the standing-rigging so the usual aft sloping mast rake is reduced or even set to rake forward will move the centre of effort of the whole rig forward, which will reduce the tendency of the boat to head into the wind when the helm is released. This is usually referred to as "weather-helm", the opposite being "lee-helm".

If this still does not have the desired effect then you are going to have to investigate more drastic measures, such as adding a bowsprit to set a larger or additional headsail or, conversely, lengthening the boom or adding a mizzen mast will reduce lee-helm. Another option is to move the mast foot forward or backwards, but this can often mean a lot of work and expense and in some cases major surgery. Before going down this road it may be wiser to reconsider the suitability of your choice of boat.

Heaving-to

Having a boat that heaves-to easily and reliably is a real advantage. How else are you going to prepare lunch? Heaving-to, which usually means sailing close to the wind and then tacking without un-cleating the headsail(s) so they become backed, ideally should result in the boat sitting comfortably and making very little way through the water. You may have to lash the helm in a particular position to achieve this state of equilibrium. Once in this position the motion will be much more comfortable and you can leave the boat to its own devices and get on with other chores or even reefing the mainsail, provided you continue to keep a good lookout.

Heaving-to on the starboard tack means that in many cases, with respect to the international rules for the prevention of collision at sea, although you may be hardly moving you are the stand-on vessel and will only need to act if another boat on port tack does not keep out of your way. Obviously, it is not appropriate to take this stance in a shipping lane.

If your boat does not heave-to satisfactorily because after a few seconds it takes charge and tacks or gibes then races off in an unpredictable direction, then you will not be able to take a break. Even if you have some form of self-steering, a hove-to yacht should give you relief from an uncomfortable motion. This is such an important consideration for the lone sailor. If you can't attend to a critical task, things can quickly get out of hand and before you know it you are in trouble.

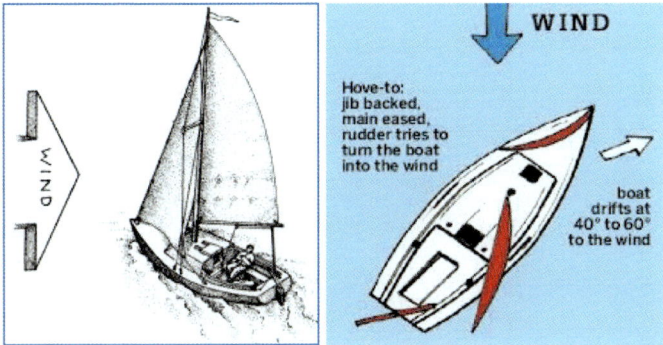

Figure 14 – a yacht can be hove-to with the headsail backed and the helm hard over

Self-tacking

If all of your sails are self-tacking, particularly when you're working in close quarters and have enough to worry about, then there are no sheets to loose or trim. You can achieve this, for example, by having boomed headsails in addition to the mainsail or just having a cat-rig with no headsail.

Tacking up a narrow channel or through moorings then becomes a simple task of just putting the helm over when it is time to tack. Don't forget that the solo yachtsperson already has one less task when tacking -- you don't need to say "ready about …….. lee-ho" in the traditional manner of alerting your crew!

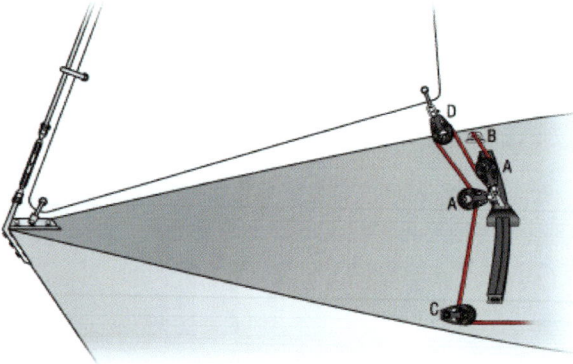

Figure 15 – an example of a sheeting arrangement for a self-tacking headsail

Fractional rigs

If you are considering going for a Bermudan rigged mainsail, you may want to consider the advantages of a fractional-rig as opposed to a masthead rig. I strongly endorse a fractional rig for many reasons.

To begin with, they have smaller headsails, which are easier and quicker to tack as there is less line to pull and less force on that line. With most of the sail area in the mainsail it is easier to sail a modern fractional rig with a minimally overlapping or non-overlapping jib, the latter being essential if you also want it to be self-tacking. If you get your timing right you can actually tack the jib on quite large fractional rigged boats without even using a winch handle if the jib does not have much overlap.

Figure 16 – fractional rig, left, and masthead, right, with its very large headsail

Of course, the mainsail is the main driving sail on a fractional rig, and modern gear allows the mainsail to be easily managed.

Also, with a fractional rig you can easily de-power the rig before you have to shorten sail. This means you can carry the same sail plan through a much wider range of wind speeds and angles. It is important on a fractional rig to have an easily adjustable backstay to adjust mast-bend as by using that backstay it takes only seconds to change from being over-powered to de-powered by flattening the sail, with no change in course and no change in actual sail trim.

To do the same with a masthead rig you have to reduce sail, typically the roller furling jib or genoa. This requires easing the jib sheet, counting on a device that usually works but in high wind situations sometimes fails to work, and then bringing in the sheet again. Once you've reefed the jib you have given up a lot of pointing performance. For the single-hander this all saps a lot of energy. However, one advantage of the masthead rig is that it is more likely you can sail to windward with just the genoa set, which is useful for the single-hander when manoeuvring in tight spaces.

Reefing

The ability to be able to shorten sail needs careful consideration by the single-handed boater. If your system means you have to repeatedly move from the cockpit to the mast, for example, the time and energy it takes increases.

Figure 17 – a yacht well reefed in a blow

Reefing is, of course, related to worsening weather and it does not help if by the time you have reduced your sail area you are physically drained and not well prepared for what is approaching.

If your reefing systems are not efficient, then as the wind continues to increase you can find yourself in a situation where you literally do not have the strength to reef and thus place yourself in danger. Waiting a while to see what happens can easily lead to a situation where reefing becomes a lot more difficult. It is often said that the time to reef is when you first think about needing to do it.

Do practice your single-handed reefing techniques in fine weather and find improvements before heading off.

You need a reefing mechanism that lends itself to working alone from a safe and secure location. Roller reefing headsails and modern two-line slab reefing on the mainsail with all lines led back to the cockpit definitely have a lot of advantages.

Fully battened mainsails, providing the mast sliders are low friction, can be an advantage by reducing the frantic sail flapping while reefing when head-to wind. If you do not have the ideal reefing system, don't give up the idea of sailing alone. But do accept the limitations and accept the fact that you need to reduce sail area much earlier. It is much better to have to shake out a reef that was put in too early when the stronger wind did not materialise, than to suffer the consequences of reefing too late.

On some boats it is possible to reef while hove-to. This may not make the process easier, but is sure does save a lot of the anxiety by keeping the boat stable and eliminating most of the noisy sail-flapping that results if you reef while head-to-wind.

Roller reefing headsails are a boon. You have to accept that the mechanism can fail, but being able to set, reef or hand a headsail with one piece of string from the cockpit is a huge advantage for the single-handed sailor.

Figure 18 – roller-reefing headsail and in-mast mainsail systems

If you do use the more traditional, and more reliable, headsail hanked on to the forestay then do consider rigging a downhaul line led back to the cockpit. Gravity alone can not always be relied on. This will ensure the sail is mostly under control before you venture to the foredeck to lash it down or change it for another size.

The twin headsails of a cutter rig means smaller individual head-sails and, if you can cope with the added complication of two halyards and another set of sheets, more scope for adjusting sail area and rig balance. Having more lines and sails does not necessarily make life harder for the single-hander if the payoff is smaller individual sail areas, which require less muscle power.

Figure 19 – a snuffer being used to tame a large cruising chute

Spinnakers, ghosters and cruising chutes, with their inherent larger sail areas, can be simply tamed with a 'snuffer'. Basically a long fabric tube with a stiff plastic collar at the lower end, these devices can be hauled down to engulf a three-corner sail into a more manageable sausage or hauled up to release and set the sail flying. You still have to go to the foredeck but won't have to share the space with a billowing sail that is trying to knock you off your feet.

The subject of sailing rigs is vast and complex as well as subjective and emotive. I have in no way completely covered the subject, but I hope I have given you the prospective single-handed sailor, some thoughts on what to consider.

"Prevention is, as in other aspects of seamanship, better than cure"

Sir Robin Knox-Johnston, the first person to complete a non-stop solo circumnavigation in his yacht 'Suhaili', between 1968 and 1969.

Chapter 3

DECK LAYOUT

Although you can do a lot to reduce the need to venture out of the cockpit on to deck, sooner or later it will be necessary and as a result the potential dangers increase. This is another case where the single-hander particularly needs to reduce the risk of an accident.

Once again we face the inevitable compromise. If you are planning to use a boat you already have or have selected one with the best hull and rig you can afford, the chances are that you will have to live with the fundamental layout of the deck. Making narrow side-decks wider or moving standing rigging that hinders your path to the fore-deck once the boat has heeled, are unlikely to be possible. But there are things you can do at a modest cost to keep you safe.

Keeping safe

All surfaces that you are likely to step on must have an adequate non-slip surface. In addition, there must be an adequately high toe-rail around the perimeter of the deck to restrain a slipping foot from going over the side into the water. Another important consideration is the position and quantity of suitable hand holds. All the above need to work at all angles of heel, not just on a fine dry day on the mooring.

Lifelines, usually in the form of plastic coated thin wires stretched between stanchions around the edge of the decks, are not regarded by everyone as essential, particularly if all the other features listed above are in place. It can be argued that lifelines on most boats are far too low to prevent a man or woman from going overboard, therefore giving a false sense of security, and can be a hazard when coming along-side or getting in or out of the tender. To be effective, lifelines should be higher than knee-height.

Figure 20 – a combined lifejacket and harness tethered by a lifeline (but the lifejacket is missing a crotch strap!)

Obviously, if you are going to sail without lifelines you need to pay extra attention to the other devices that are going to keep you out of the water. Wearing a safety harness, preferably integrated into a lifejacket worn at all times, which is tethered via a safety-line to jackstays running the length of the boat, is highly recommended. However, care needs to be taken to ensure they keep you on the deck.

Jackstays usually consist of ropes, wires or webbing-straps fastened to bow and stern and lying along each side-deck to which you clip one end of your standard two metre long safety-line with the other end attached to your harness. The safety-line clip then runs along the jackstay as you move from one end of the boat to the other.

Although this arrangement will keep you attached to the boat should you fall overboard, it is far better to be kept in the dry in the first place. If the jackstays are on or close to the centreline of the boat and the safety-line less than half the boat's beam in length you will be far safer. If they are apt to be walked on, then webbing-straps are best as they do not roll underfoot. Some safety-lines have an additional hook halfway along so you can easily change from a long to short line.

Jackstays should also not extend the full length of the boat but stop a little less than safety-line length from the bow and stop far enough from the stern so you can get back on board and not be towed helplessly two metres behind your boat.

Even if you have all of the above, in order to climb back on board you must have a fixed boarding ladder or some other system that can be deployed by someone in the water. A simple idea is to have steps incorporated into the rudder if it is transom-hung.

Sail controls at the mast or in the cockpit?
Some sailors prefer having sail control lines and halyards at the mast and others think that leading them back to the

cockpit is better. Obviously, this debate is of no consequence if you have a small or open boat where the mast can be reached from the cockpit. For boats where you have to leave the safety of a cockpit to venture over the deck to the mast it can be safer to lead all control lines and halyards aft.

The trade-off is extra friction, requiring more effort and a lot of extra line in the cockpit. However, both of these disadvantages can be largely overcome by providing stowage bags for the lines and by using modern low friction ball-bearing blocks.

Headsails on roller reefing or furling systems and mainsails with in-mast roller reefing do not need their halyards led back because with these arrangements the sails are seldom lowered at sea. Therefore, it makes sense to have just the associated reefing and furling lines led to the cockpit.

Figure 21 – lines need to be well organised!

Hanked on headsails can have the halyard and a downhaul line led aft but you will still have to go forward to tie down the sail or, rarely seen these days, tie in the reef points.

Mainsails with slab reefing or boom roller reefing will need all halyards, reefing lines and the topping lift either operated at the mast or all led to the cockpit. You cannot have, for instance, reefing lines at the mast and halyards led back, or any other combination, as this achieves nothing. You are unlikely to be able to reef without making repeated trips between mast and cockpit. Also, with a slab-reefed main, you will still have to venture on deck to apply the sail-ties once the sail is lowered, unless you also have a self-stowing system.

An option is to have the mainsail halyard led back to the cockpit, with the reefing lines controlled at the mast, providing you can put the halyard around a winch and take it with you when you go to the mast to reef. A spare cleat will be needed at the mast to secure the halyard but once the reef is complete you then take the halyard back to the cockpit to finish tensioning the luff.

My own preference for my slab-reefed main is to have everything at the mast for simplicity, but also to use a safety harness for personal safety.

Snags

The biggest problem here is the danger of sheets getting caught on protuberances when sails are flapping and the sheets flailing. This can happen during hoisting, lowering, reefing, tacking or gybing.

Few things are more dangerous for a single-hander than trying to free a jib sheet that has snagged a mast mounted winch while the boat is rolling in a seaway. If you are going to be using your existing boat for your first solo voyage then you should already know where snags occur.

In the past with crew to help, it may not have been much of a problem, but now you must devise a way of avoiding the problem. If the object that catches the sheet can be moved or removed all together, then this is the best solution. Failing that, you need to fit either a guide or shield so the sheet has nothing to catch on. In some cases just a simple line stretched across the foredeck will prevent the sheets from snagging the mooring cleats. But you have to accept that this will result in a trip hazard.

Going aloft

Although being able to climb your mast is not essential to sailing a boat, even with crew, if you want to be self-reliant and able to rectify most problems yourself, sooner or later something will happen that necessitates a trip to the masthead. There are many methods of scaling a mast, but most of them require a degree of team-work. Alone, your options are limited but by far the best option is not to do it while underway.

Those spending many days or weeks away from land may need to sort out a problem aloft in order to continue to make progress. The coastal sailor, however, by definition is never far from help, so the best option is to get to a harbour or marina. Once there you then have the choice of climbing the mast more safely on your own or seeking someone to help you.

If your boat is small and light enough, hauling on a line from the masthead while on a beach or in a marina will bring the masthead down to you. This technique is known as careening.

Going aloft alone

Do not try this while at sea! If you really need to go up the mast without assistance, then the following methods are suggested: (1) three part tackle, (2) ascenders and (3) ladders. My favourite is the three-part tackle with a double ball-bearing block at the top, hoisted aloft on a halyard, and a single ball-bearing block with becket, attached to your bosun's chair.

Ideally, the lower block should be a ratchet type as this makes a significant difference to the effort needed to hold your position between pulls or to take a breather. Flick the ratchet switch to the "off" position for a smooth descent. Leather sailing gloves of the type with cut-off thumb and forefinger avoid skin abrasion.

Figure 22 –ascending a mast using a bosun's chair and a three-part tackle

Although in theory this 3:1 ratio tackle means you need only one third of the effort (plus the effort to overcome friction) to raise a given weight, in practice, because you are reducing your own weight on the bosun's chair each time you pull on the line, the effort required is less.

As you go up, you need to stuff the free end of the rope into a bag fitted to you or your bosun's chair. If you let the free end just fall to the deck it could get snagged, preventing you from being able to lower yourself back down. Once you are at your chosen height you need to tie off the free end to leave your hands free. This is best done by taking a bight in the hauling part, passing it under the shackle of your bosun's chair, then up and making two half hitches around the tackle just above the lower block.

If all the above sounds too complicated, then you should either forget the whole idea of going aloft without any help or consider the following alternatives.

Ascending with mechanical ascenders

You can climb a halyard, stretched taught between masthead and deck, using two mechanical ascenders (sometimes called Jumars™, which is just a brand name).

Figure 23 – a pair of mechanical ascenders can be used for mast climbing

One way to use ascenders is simply to attach both to the rope, clip each of them to your harness with slings, and then attach a length of line to each with a loop in the end. Stick one foot into one loop and the other foot into the other, and up you go, transferring your weight from foot to foot and sliding the ascenders up one at a time.

Ascending with two friction knots

If you do not want to purchase mechanical ascenders or are worried about the wear they can inflict on your halyards, perhaps the next most common method is to employ two friction knots, for example, prusiks. Tie the first prusik to the halyard and clip this to your harness. Tie a second prusik (from a longer loop of cord) to the rope, form a slip knot in its tail and put one foot through the slip knot.

Figure 24 – use of friction knots as a climbing aid

Now simply stand up on the foot prusik and, once the harness prusik is un-loaded, slide it up as high as you can reach. Sit down and place your weight on the harness prusik once more, and then slide the foot prusik up a comfortable distance. Stand up, and repeat the whole process over and over again. It can take quite some time and can be somewhat tiring but it does get you up there.

Figure 25 – a prusik knot

The klemheist knot is often used instead of a prusik knot because it does not tighten on the rope as much as a prusik knot, and thereby allows the climber to move the knot more easily.

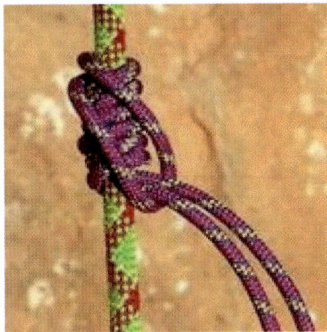

Figure 26 – a Klemheist knot

Mast ladders and steps

Another method is to use a mast ladder, a number of which are available. They are usually flexible and slot into the mainsail luff groove in the mast, then hoisted aloft with a halyard. (e.g. see www.mastmate.com). These are no good on a traditional gaff rigged boat that does not have a luff groove in the mast, but are highly effective on almost all types of Bermudian rigged craft if you have the (sometimes significant) space to stow them when not in use.

Figure 27 – mast ladders that locate in the luff groove and are hoisted aloft

Permanent steps attached to the mast, either fixed or folding, have their advantages, as do ratlines on the shrouds, but they add weight and windage aloft which will significantly affect performance on the smaller yacht. With a gaff rig you can climb the luff of the mainsail while it is up using the luff lacing or hoops as footholds. However, neither this method nor ratlines will likely allow you to reach the masthead, more often the location of the problem that needs attention.

With any mast climbing system, you must have a back-up safety line attaching a separate harness to a second halyard using, for example, a prusik knot. Do practice using this kit while other people are available to help should something go wrong and do rehearse how you would get down should the system fail and you end up hanging from the back-up line.

All other aspects and considerations of deck layout are the same, no matter how many crew are on board.

Chapter 4

BELOW-DECK LAYOUT

Another advantage of sailing solo is that you get more space to stow all your gear, but the obvious down-side is having no one to help you find something quickly. You do need to be more organised about how and where things needed during a voyage are stowed, particularly those items you may need in a hurry when you have only one hand free.

Figure 28 – a well organised and tidy cabin

While extra clothing, food and drink all need to be stowed close to the companionway, having all your navigation equipment and charts stored below may not be ideal. Being able to see your charts, echo-sounder, GPS, etc., from the helm is preferable to having to spend time in the cabin. Most electronic devices are waterproof and charts can either be kept in a clear plastic sleeve or purchased in weatherproof material. All this will allow you to do much of your navigation and pilotage underway without having to keep going below.

Time spent down below while sailing in rougher conditions can lead to sea-sickness. Even if this does not normally affect you, there are times when even the hardiest sailor can succumb. Motion-sickness is a serious problem to the lone sailor. For most people keeping an eye on the horizon or the shoreline usually does the trick. So, being in the cabin for very long is not a good idea during rough water.

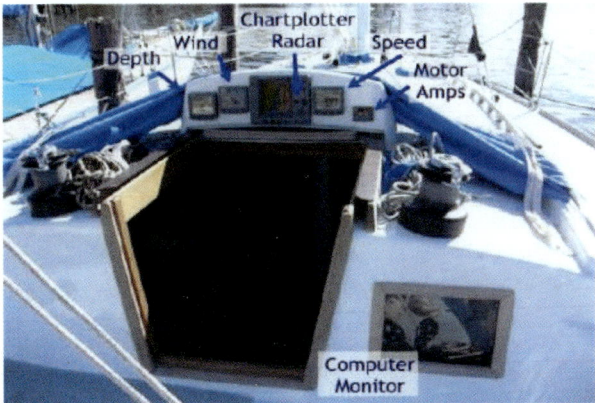

Figure 29 – instruments and the chart viewable from the helm and with other supplies stored easy to hand just inside the companionway

Of course, if you are sailing an open boat this chapter has the wrong title, but this is all about having your gear well organised and stowed. It is also about being able to easily reach the important things and being able to do important tasks like finding and putting on warmer clothes while underway.

You also need to have adequate dry stowage. If a wave breaks and sends a dollop of cold water into the cockpit and down your neck you need to act quickly, before the cold water starts to chill your body and affect your dexterity.

So, after stabilising the boat by heaving-to, you need to remove clothing, quickly find a dry set, re-dress and take command of the ship again before something else happens that needs your attention. This can be done only if you know exactly where your kit is stowed and is stowed so it stays dry until needed.

Everything below that is not in a locker must be well secured, so that after being hit by a large wave you can still find everything. Items on shelves or worktops, even if these have high fiddles, may still benefit from straps or netting to restrain them.

In short, the single-hander needs to be well organised and tidy.

"The chance for mistakes is about equal to the number of crew squared"

Ted Turner, an avid competitive sailor who won the 1977 America's Cup.

Chapter 5

SAFETY EQUIPMENT

Standard lists of minimum recommended safety equipment are produced by a number of authorities such as the Royal Yachting Association (see Appendix 1 for a full list). However, there are a number of items that need specific consideration for the lone sailor.

VHF radio

Can you operate the VHF radio while steering? Imagine approaching a marina and needing to talk to the berthing master while you are negotiating a busy or tricky entrance. Not something a self-steering system can help you with. If you really can't position a fixed VHF radio so you can operate it from the cockpit, then consider having an additional hand-held VHF. This would make an ideal backup to the fixed set but not ideal as the only one on board due to its reduced range versus a fixed set.

Steering systems

Although standard safety equipment lists often include the need for secondary steering mechanisms should the primary one fail, the single-hander should also have a hands-free means of operating the primary steering.

Relying 100% on the electric autopilot is no good because they are not totally robust. Tiller mounted autopilots, in particular, are not all completely waterproof (despite what the manufacturers would have you believe), so heavy rain or a splash of seawater can destroy the inner workings in seconds. The more expensive autopilots have their electronics and compasses (the more sensitive parts) mounted in a separate container that can be positioned in a less vulnerable location, but most yachtsmen use the self-contained tiller-mounted autopilot, which is not so well protected.

A good way of reducing the risk of water ingress is to have a waterproof jacket for the autopilot that will shed most of the water and spray. I have not found one of these commercially available, but it is not difficult to make one from an off-cut of sail cover material such as "Topgun" or even the sleeve of an old sailing jacket.

Figure 30 – an autopilot with "jacket" for additional protection from water ingress

An excellent addition to the autopilot for the lone sailor is the wireless remote control. With this palm-size device attached to your harness with a lanyard, you can adjust the boat's heading by pressing its buttons irrespective of where you are on deck. For example, if you are at the mast about to drop the mainsail with the autopilot on and the engine driving slow ahead and the wind shifts, just a few button presses will restore the status quo. Without this device you would have to re-cleat the halyard, go back to the cockpit, adjust the heading and return to the mast to continue with the operation. A wireless remote control spares you all that.

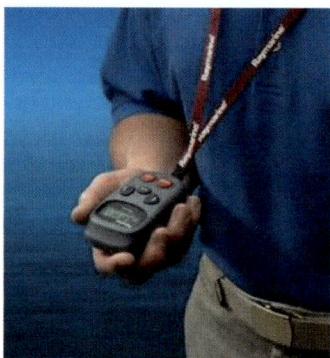

Figure 31 – a wireless remote control for an autopilot (photograph by Raymarine)

Keeping a look-out

It should go without saying that for your own safety you need to keep a look-out for other vessels. In fact, the International Regulations for the Prevention of Collision at Sea states: *"Every vessel shall at all times maintain a proper look-out by sight and hearing as well as by all available means appropriate in the prevailing circumstances and conditions so as to make a full appraisal of the situation and of the risk of collision."*

With only one set of eyes on board and many distractions from the process of sailing and navigating the boat you may want to consider other devices. Radar, radar detectors and

AIS (Automatic Identification System) are such devices and they really come into their own in reduced visibility as they are largely immune to fog and darkness.

Radar lets you "see" solid objects and can have "guard zones" set so an alarm will sound if something is getting too close. Less hungry of electrical energy, a radar detector will audibly warn you of another vessel in the vicinity that has an active radar set. These passive radar detectors can display the relative bearing of any vessel operating radar within the range of the antenna's horizon and produce a tone each time it receives a signal. Obviously, this device has its limitations, but can certainly reduce the risk of collision.

The more recent innovation and a very effective device for detecting the position of shipping is AIS, the Automatic Identification System. The AIS is a very good substitute for radar on a small boat with limited battery capacity and a limited budget. AIS works by continuously transmitting a ship's identity on VHF radio frequencies -- position, speed and course, along with other relevant information -- to all other AIS equipped vessels within range.

AIS transponders on other vessels and coast stations receive this information and use it to build up a live graphical display of traffic in the area. The receiver can be connected to many types of chart plotter or PC charting software.

Since 2004, an AIS must be fitted aboard all ships of 300 gross tonnage and upwards engaged in international voyages, cargo ships of 500 gross tonnage and upwards not engaged in international voyages and all passenger ships irrespective of size. So AIS is really effective in areas where there is a lot of large commercial shipping.

Yachts can alternatively fit a receiver-only type AIS, using less power at a more affordable price but lacking the ability to transmit your presence to other vessels. This type at least allows you to keep more clear of the big boys, always a good idea and certainly a better strategy than assuming they can identify you and will give way.

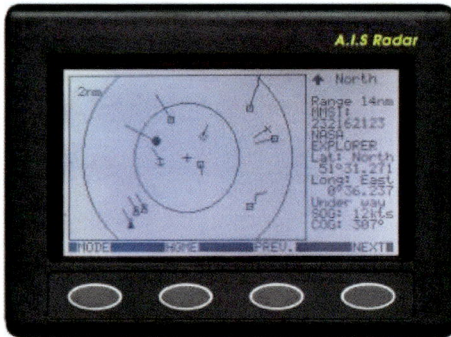

Figure 32 – a basic AIS display screen showing the relative position and track of shipping

AIS is not a substitute for a radar, but can offer similar capabilities and even enhance a radar image if a radar has already been fitted to the vessel, and the data from them both are superimposed on the same screen. The system also has the advantage of the VHF radio signals, within limits, travelling around bends and over land giving better coverage than radar or enhancing a radar picture when used together.

Man-overboard!

Why is there is not much call for man-overboard equipment such a life-belts, throw-lines and dan-buoys on the single-hander's boat? Because no one will be there to yell "Man Overboard", turn the boat round and pick you out of the water. Do not, I repeat, do not fall overboard. Do everything you can to reduce the chance of falling overboard.

The subject of life-lines, jack-lines and handholds has already been covered in chapter 3

If despite all of your precautions you do end up in the water, then you need buoyancy and you need help. Fast. Sailors who sail solo far from land have said there is no point in wearing a lifejacket as it will only prolong your death once you are in the water and your boat has sailed away. It would be nice to hear the views of those that did go over the side without one! They may have given different advice. Personally, I always wear an automatic gas-inflation lifejacket with integral harness.

Figure 33 – a personal locator beacon (PLB) which can be stowed in a pouch attached to your lifejacket

Personal Location Beacons (PLBs) that transmit on the 406 MHz global satellite rescue system are getting smaller and more affordable, so consider having one of these fixed to your person. Although they also transmit a 121.5MHz homing signal, the type containing a GPS satellite receiver will ensure the rescue services find you sooner, possibly within 30 minutes, versus one or two hours for one without GPS. Wearing typical sailing clothes and a lifejacket, in UK waters, you are unlikely to survive hypothermia after an hour in the water. With the advent of lower cost GPS almost all PLBs on the market today contain a GPS.

Alternatively, as you are most likely to be within VHF radio range of the rescue services or other vessels, one of the new breed of small waterproof hand-held VHF radios fixed to your lifejacket could be a lifesaver.

Do please think about how you attach a PLB or VHF to your belt, harness or lifejacket. Once in the water and your lifejacket has self-inflated, creating a bulbous balloon about your neck and chest that restricts your head movement and arm articulation and your visibility, will you still be able to reach for the device and be able to operate it?

Knife

You should already be aware of the importance of having a sharp knife handy for cutting ropes in an emergency, but for the solo sailor "handy" means "within reach". Ideally you should always have one about your body. You could have a pen-knife on a lanyard in a pocket but unless it is of the sprung-loaded type these are very difficult to open if you only have one hand free. Better to have a fixed blade knife in a sheath. I also keep a fixed blade knife sitting in a holster just by the companionway for instant use in the cockpit.

Bilge pump

Can you operate the manual bilge pump while steering? With no one to lend a hand both tasks fall to you. If you are desperately trying to sail off a lee shore to escape the rock that has just cracked your hull after a collision with your keel, it is no good if all you can do is watch the water level rise.

An electric bilge pump could be a good investment but should not be a substitute for an easy access manual one in reach of the helm. Remember that by the time you have realised you have too much water inside the boat, your batteries may already be awash.

The anchor

How quickly can you let go the anchor? If something goes wrong and you find yourself drifting towards shallow water or land, one of your options is to drop the hook in an attempt to maintain your position and avert disaster. With no crew to help, your anchor is useless if it is stowed at the bottom of a locker with a heap of rope and fenders on top. All but the smallest of boats should carry a second anchor. Is that, too, ready to be quickly deployed?

First aid

No matter how well we look after them, our bodies occasionally let us down or accidentally get damaged. Illness or injury can leave you in serious trouble. You are the captain of the ship but have to do everything with no one else to rely on. Obviously, prevention is better than cure, but should the worst happen then you need to have some remedies to hand for the more likely problems.

When you need your first-aid kit you have to be able to find it easily and quickly. I recommend three watertight plastic containers clearly marked on the outside. One containing dressings, one medication and the other with the basics for saving someone else's life. If you are not clear on what should be in the latter box then I recommend you attend a first aid course.

In general, the actual contents of the first-aid kit will be the same as that for the crewed yacht.

In many cases you will be able to treat wounds (damage to the surface of the skin) yourself by thoroughly cleaning the area and applying a dressing to stop blood loss and prevent infection. If bleeding continues, do not remove the dressing; just put another one on top. Anything that gets into your eyes should be flushed out with copious amounts of fresh water. Burns should be immediately cooled under running cold water for at least 10 minutes. If necessary, use sea-water! Do not apply any ointment and although it is preferable not to apply a dressing, if really necessary, wrap clean cling-film or a plastic bag over the burn first to stop the dressing sticking.

If you get stung by an insect try to remove any sting left in the skin as soon as possible, but avoid using tweezers as these can squeeze more poison into you. Instead, scrape the skin with the edge of a credit card. If you start to feel ill or get swelling or itching anywhere else, then call for help quickly in case you are having an allergic reaction to the sting.

Never underestimate the effects of sun-stroke or heat exhaustion, even in the UK. Once it has taken hold you will not be able to treat yourself and probably will not be well enough to sail safely. It is important that you wear a hat, use abundant sun-screen lotion and drink plenty of water to ensure you do not suffer in the first place.

Figure 34 –dressed for protection from the sun

There is not much more than the above that you can do on your own. It is difficult to treat yourself and in some cases almost impossible to accurately diagnose your problem when you are ill and your brain is not processing at its best.

Call for help early before the situation deteriorates. I expect most countries have a similar service but, here in the UK, all you need to do is call "UK Coastguard" on VHF channel 16 or by mobile-phone (call 999 or 112 and ask for the

Coastguard). You can then request to be put through to a duty doctor for advice.

Eyesight

If your eyesight is not adequate to read charts or identify distant navigation buoys without glasses, it is essential that you have spare spectacles because no matter how well they are strapped on, a flailing rope can whisk them away in a flash. Even contact lenses are not infallible. If you cannot make out the light characteristics of a navigation buoy printed on a chart, your position may be in doubt.

Sailing single-handed means you cannot ask your crew to read the small-print for you so a backup is essential. If you can manage with your previous prescription spectacles, then keep them on board, otherwise you will have to invest in a second pair. If you only need them for reading then a cheap off-the-shelf pair from the local chemist or drug-store will do the job.

Do not think you can use the prescription sun-glasses that your optician gave free as a second pair because they are dangerous if you need to use them at night. Even photochromic lenses, the type that darken in sunlight, are not safe to use when sailing after sunset.

The April 2007 UK's Marine Accident Investigation Branch report, on the investigation of the loss of the sailing yacht "Ouzo" and her three crew south of the Isle of Wight in August 2006 when it was run down in the night by a ferry bound for Spain, concluded that a probable contributory factor was that the ferry's lookout was wearing spectacles with photochromic lenses. The report stated that the optical transmission of these lenses were less than 80% efficient, compared to 95 to 99% for ordinary lenses.

"It is better to travel alone than with a bad companion".

African Proverb.

Chapter 6

ORGANISATION

If something goes wrong the resourceful sailor will find a solution. If a second unexpected thing happens before you get a chance to fix the first, you will be hard pressed and need to organise things quickly. And if then a normally minor problem happens to be the third in succession, things can rapidly get out of hand, putting you in serious trouble as the problems accumulate and the situation deteriorates.

This is where good organisation counts. If you can diagnose a problem quickly, know what to do and where the equipment is to fix it and fix it efficiently, then you will not leave yourself open to accumulating issues, damage management, and possible disaster. Don't forget you are doing this for enjoyment so time spent planning organised and logical stowage is essential. Everything should be to hand where and when you need it.

When hand steering is necessary, make sure everything that might be needed for the duration is within easy reach of the helm before starting out. On boats with a tiller, adding an extension or running control lines forward will increase your range of movement. Unless circumstances prohibit it, take a short break periodically and move around, even if it means having to heave-to or temporarily alter course to a point where the boat can sail itself with the tiller/wheel locked. You never know when a situation may arise that will prevent you from leaving the helm and you want to be as fresh and alert as possible if it does.

Have a number of small torches placed around the boat. Even if you are not planning any night sailings, if you are sleeping on board and need to find a spare fuse for the anchor light you need to be able to see into your spares locker without wasting time searching in the other end of the boat for the single torch.

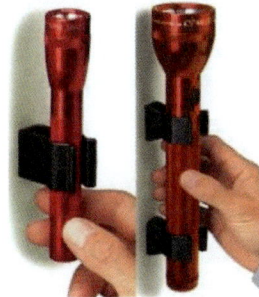

Figure 35 – small torches fixed in various places around the cabin are very useful when searching in the dark

I find that the small AA size of Maglight™ or equivalent, held in a clip or a Velcro fastening, works well and always works even after being on board for years due to their watertight seals.

On the subject of lights, my favourite is a tiny LED head-light made by Petzl™ (http://www.petzl.com/en/Sport/Lighting?l=INT). With one of these on your head you can move around the cabin or the deck with both hands free and have enough light to do any job within the length of the boat. You might even forget it is actually dark until you switch it off and are shocked to see just how black it actually is. The beam may not be adequate to see more than 10m away, but for moving around on board and all other work tasks these lights are great.

Figure 36 – An LED head-light - small, light and a long battery life

The light from these LEDs will, however, highlight the reflective patches on the masthead wind indicator even on a tall mast.

Although I do not know why, the light emitted from LEDs does not seem so detrimental to night-time vision once you turn them off, unlike the light from traditional incandescent bulbs.

What happens if….

The toughest part of single-handing is reacting when something goes wrong -- the autopilot dies, the mainsail luff jams in it's groove, the furling line overrides the drum and locks up, or water from an unknown source is coming into the boat, all of which might happen while you need to keep a lookout or hand-steer the boat.

Picture what might happen if all of a sudden smoke starts coming up from below while motoring up a narrow channel through lines of moorings. Or simple things like discovering that the marina manager on the VHF radio was mistaken and the berth you're pulling into in 30 seconds isn't a port tie up after all and your fenders and lines are on the wrong side and the fairway you're in is too narrow for you to spin around. All a lot easier to cope with if there are extra hands on board. But on your own you need to plan to avoid getting into these situations.

Always putting fenders and lines on both sides may take a few minutes longer before you enter a marina, but it saves a whole lot of last minute worry or even a damaged boat. If you do not have enough, go buy some now.

A final word on organisation

It is important to ensure all equipment and machinery is well maintained and regularly inspected for any wear or deterioration. There is a lot to be said for keeping things simple but most boats will have an engine and a number of devices connected to an electrical supply. If you are reliant on any of these systems to get you to your destination or to get you into port then they need to be dependable. Ensue you are up to date on all maintenance and you do regular visual checks to spot anything that is deteriorating. This will reduce the chances of an unexpected failure.

Make sure everything, especially safety equipment, spares and tools, is all stowed where you can find it quickly so you can fix a problem fast before something else goes wrong and compounds the situation. Be organised. A place for everything and everything in its place.

"The charm of single-handed cruising is not solitude, but independence."

Claud Worth, author of Yacht Cruising and of Yacht Navigation and Voyaging.

Chapter 7

HUMAN LIMITATIONS

Most tasks you can accomplish alone. They may take more time but you've got lots of time when single-handing and you can avoid most risks with proper training, equipment and planning. Lack of an extra set of hands, eyes, ears, and mind can be a matter of safety, but is usually just an inconvenience. All you need to do is to work within your limitations once you have established what those limitations are!

Sleep/endurance/fatigue

The UK's Marine Accident Investigation Board (MAIB) recently noted that in an analysis of 65 marine incidents over a 10 year period, one-third of the groundings involved a fatigued officer alone on the bridge at night, two-thirds of the vessels involved in collisions were not keeping a proper lookout, and one-third of all the accidents that occurred at night involved a sole watch-keeper on the bridge. (Source: NUMAST (2006), Fatigue: IMO Must Act, NUMAST Telegraph, March 2006, p.40.).

As a lone sailor with no one to share the workload or give you a break, there will be a limit to how long you can sail without a rest. Some claim they can go for 24 hours, a few even 30, without sleep. Everyone is different, so the answer is to understand what causes fatigue, how it affects your abilities and endurance. Then, plan your voyages accordingly to ensure you remain safe. Just because others can stay awake for 30 hours does not mean that you can.

Our body functions run on a repeated 24-26 hour cycle and we normally sleep at a regular time during the night. Because our body clock is partly controlled by what we do, as well as by daylight, we can change our body clock a bit. For example, if you normally go to bed at 8 p.m. and get up at 3 a.m. you have adjusted your body clock a bit earlier than most people.

If you are a regular night-shift worker your body clock will partly change so that you get some sleep during the day and work reasonably well at night. But you can not change your body clock to become a totally night person, because the presence of daylight stops the clock from being changed that much. Sleep is a part of life. Sleep is what really cures fatigue and sufficient sleep prevents fatigue.

Most people report sleeping around seven and a half hours a day. Some sleep less than this during the night and make up for it in naps. But don't think naps are a substitute for six hours of continuous sleep at night. Naps can be used to supplement a good sleep at night and help prevent sleep debt, but they are not as beneficial as a good sleep at night. Sleep debt is the accumulation of fatigue from several days with inadequate sleep. Sleep debt can be calculated by adding together the hours of sleep lost each day compared to your normal sleep. Losing two hours of sleep each day for four days will make you nearly as fatigued as losing one whole night of sleep. Plan your voyage to ensure you have committed time for enough hours of sleep to cancel the debt.

You can work out the amount of sleep you really need by taking a week of regular sleep of six hours each night. See how you feel with six hours sleep. Then, take a few days of six and a half hours of sleep. How do you feel now? Better? Increase your sleep by another half hour for a few days.

When you no longer get any more benefit from increasing your sleep period, you have established how much sleep you really need. Caffeine in coffee and cola is an excellent mild stimulant, but you will rapidly get used to it if you use it all the time. If you use stimulants, remember to use them only when you really need them, and when sleep is not an option.

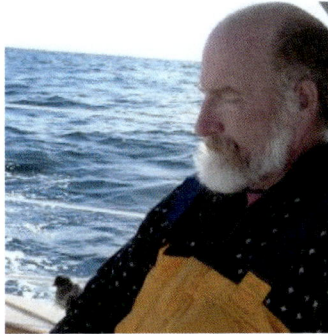

Figure 37 – sleeping underway is not recommended – even with nothing in sight you could be in danger in less than 10 minutes

It is possible to take many "mini-sleeps" of 15 to 20 minutes at a time. Various alarms can be used to awaken the skipper, and upon wakening the routine is to check for traffic, check boat speed and sail trim, make a check of navigation and boat condition and then back you go for another sleep cycle.

For long passages away from land and out of shipping lanes this may be an acceptable risk. However, for the coastal sailor the amount of time you can afford to be off duty will be very short. Land and shallow water may not be far away and the presence of fishing boats, commercial carriers and even other yachts plying the coast are ever frequent hazards to be avoided. Even if you can see nothing on the horizon, from the deck of a small boat an inshore fishing boat may not be seen until it is less than 3 miles away. With a closing speed of 15 knots you will only have 10 minutes before you need to take emergency action to avoid a collision.

Sea-sickness

As an experienced sailor hopefully you will already know if you are susceptible to sea-sickness. Even if this only happens to you on rare occasions it is worth thinking about some strategies to cope should the worst happen when alone. Don't delay. Even though you hope it will go away again, it rarely does unless you do something to change the motion of the boat or to focus your mind on another task. Changing course towards sheltered water or to a different angle to the wind, heaving to, or making a conscious effort to study the type and motion of every other boat around you. Whatever you do, do it at the first signs while you are able to think straight and rationally!

Food and drink

Obviously we need food and water to sustain life, but getting enough to sustain strength and endurance as well as warding off dehydration when you are fully occupied managing a boat is a challenge.

Luckily, the coastal sailor does not have to prepare and cook meals if conditions are not suitable because having ready-prepared meals, snacks and drinks will keep your body supplied. Local shops or supermarkets offer readymade sandwiches, pasties, pasta salads, etc. Cooking a more substantial meal can wait until you are safely in a haven. The need to reach shelter will be dictated sooner by the needs of sleep than by the need to cook a meal. Having a supply of bottled water on board that can be reached from the cockpit it essential to ensure you keep hydrated. The situation is completely different when crossing oceans, but that is not the subject of this book.

The basic advice is to plan ahead for each passage and have everything at hand. If the weather forecast is good for an easy passage, preparing a meal and cooking while underway will be possible in most boats. However, always have something instant as backup in case things do not work out as planned. Depriving yourself of food and drink for too long can also affect your mental state and lead to making bad decisions.

If the conditions are right and you decide to cook while underway, then do try to prepare something a bit special that you enjoy. After all, you will not have to worry about the tastes or fads of anyone else on board!

Using the heads

I am not going to dwell on this subject for long except to say that you need to have a plan. If your self-steering arrangement will not keep the boat out of trouble for long enough, you need to change to a more suitable course where it will or you will have to heave-to. With no self-steering on a boat that will not heave-to you are going to have to be inventive unless you can keep all your passages within your critical retention span.

Men may think they have an easy option of standing at the rail and peeing down-wind, but this presents an unacceptable risk of falling overboard. Please do not do this unless securely restrained. The conventional two metre long harness lifeline may keep you attached to the boat, but trying to get back on board while being dragged along in the water will quickly sap your strength and may result in tragedy. There will be no one to throw you a lifebelt or haul you back on board.

Using a bucket or other suitably sized container in the cockpit so you are close to the controls and able to keep a lookout is eminently preferable to doing it over the side or spending too long below in the heads.

You also need to consider your foul weather clothing. It is no good if these are so impractical that you need to strip them off completely every time, resulting in excessive exposure to the weather and too long not under command of your vessel. Packs of baby-wipes, as used by parents to clean little bottoms on the go, are great for quick and easy hand washing afterwards.

The tender

Unless you can always step on or off your boat directly from land you will need a tender/dinghy. The main consideration here for the single-hander is the limitation of your own strength to launch and recover one either from the shore or from your boat, particularly after a tiring passage.

Whether you have, or prefer, a rigid or inflatable tender with or without wheels or an outboard engine there will probably be a difference when there is no one else to help you. Towing the tender while underway means you do not have to lift it aboard, otherwise, unless you have davits or a winching system you need a tender sufficiently light for you to lift it on deck for stowage or deflation. When you go ashore if you need to get the tender up a beach or slipway there may not be someone close by to assist if you can't manage alone.

A few manufacturers make inflatables that are significantly lighter than the average. Although I have not tried one, several people have recommended to me the "superlight" ones from "3D Tender" (http://www.3dtender.com). With one of these you are more likely to be able to lift or carry it.

No matter how short the distance from mooring to shore, do wear your lifejacket. Many more yachtsmen/women drown in the tender than their yacht.

Not always alone

Humans are social animals. We enjoy companionship, being in the company of others and sharing experiences, sights and thoughts. But "alone" does not necessarily mean lonely. While at sea, a single-handed skipper can interact with others by radio.

When coastal cruising, the desire for companionship is easily met in ports and anchorages. Boaters are a hospitable group and seem especially welcoming to a single-hander. You will not be short of comrades once you arrive in port.

"The pessimist complains about the wind; the optimist expects it to change; the realist adjusts the sails."

William A. Ward

Chapter 8

PASSAGE PLANNING

Planning a passage is very much the same process for the lone sailor as for the skipper of the fully crewed yacht. Gathering together all the charts, weather forecasts and tide tables, considering crew experience and boat capabilities, working out where and when you can safely sail to within all the constraints, investigating contingencies and letting someone ashore know your plans, should be the same tasks every time you venture out.

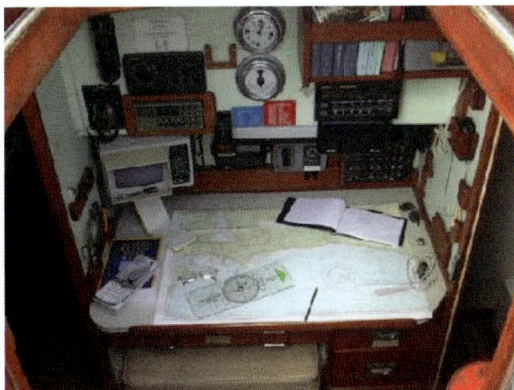

Figure 38 – a chart table with a well assembled compilation of notes, data and pilot books in readiness for a voyage

The only difference when sailing solo is that you need to be more thorough in gathering all the information into one place in an easily consultable format. The reason is that the single-hander has to do all the work once underway. If you need to refer to the plan or review one of your contingencies, it is not ideal if you then have to start referring to the index in the almanac for the appropriate page or rummaging through every chart to find the correct one.

All this extra work is wasteful of your time resource and can lead to mistakes. You have no one else to share the workload or to double-check your decisions, so make good use of the time you dedicate to planning before you depart.

You should either copy all the relevant pages in the almanac and pilot book and put them into a singe binder, or put markers into the pages of the books. Yellow post-its sticking out, with your written notes on them, work well. Charts should be stacked in the expected order you will need them.

Arrivals

Perhaps the only aspect of a passage plan that needs even more attention by the solo sailor is the subject of arrival. What will happen on arrival at a mooring, harbour or marina needs careful research and planning because his is when you will have the most tasks to perform in a short period of time. It makes no sense to have a harbour in your contingency plan as a safe haven for when you have to shorten the voyage due to bad weather, only to be surprised that there is no suitable sheltered area to get your sails down before entering. You need to do thorough research and think everything through before you set out and only plan to enter that harbour in fine weather.

If all or part of your voyage is at night and you have a choice, it is safer to *start* in the dark than to *arrive* in the dark.

Another small but important task is to write down the VHF radio channel numbers you may need on arrival, such as those for the harbour-master or lock-keeper. Communicating with them just before arrival will make for a much smoother operation, particularly if you tell them you are alone. So take the time to find and write down the correct channel numbers before you set out.

Figure 39 – you need to prepare particularly well for your arrival when you will probably be tired and exhausted

Be aware that at the end of a passage you are more likely to be suffering from fatigue and therefore less able to perform jobs quickly and more likely to make mistakes. It's all down to you, so plan well and give yourself the time and space to do a good job.

Although you should not rely solely on your GPS, or any other electronic equipment for that matter, these satellite navigation devices can significantly reduce your workload, as well as your uncertainty and worry about your position. Yes, you must still plan your route, plot your waypoints and track your position and progress on up-to-date paper charts, but if you can afford a GPS then do make full use of it. Any tool that enables you to spend more time keeping a good look-out must be a good thing when you have fewer eyes on board.

Remember to make a note of how many miles you can cover with the fuel you have on board should there be no wind or the wind unexpectedly dies on-route.

"It takes several years for anyone to learn to handle a yacht reasonably well, and a lifetime to admit how much more there is to learn."

Maurice Griffiths (1902 to 1997), a noted yachtsman, boat designer and writer on sailing subjects.

Chapter 9

BOAT/SAIL HANDLING

The process of casting off, sailing to another location and mooring up is what we yachtsmen or yachtswomen all do for pleasure. Yes, I know, there are occasions when the weather and the sea state are not as expected and we question our choice of sport, but those are the times we try to forget. Sailing from A to B is what we do, with or without helpful crew, and the process of operating the boat and the sailing rig, although a complex one, is something we face.

However, this book is not for the beginner sailor, so in this chapter I will again remain focused on those aspects specific to the single-hander. As I have stated in previous chapters, when on your own most tasks are easily performed with good forward planning so as to give yourself enough time and space to do multiple tasks in a logical sequence. Ignore this important planning and you end up unable to do multiple tasks simultaneously. If you find yourself rushing or trying to do too much at once you will not enjoy yourself and possibly put yourself in danger. As a result you will not be sailing for pleasure but rather for self preservation!

Sheet positions

When helming each sail sheet should be within reach. If you get a gust of wind and need to quickly release a sheet to prevent your boat heeling excessively it is no good if you need to leave the helm and take three paces forward to do so.

There are some yachts on the market with wheel steering and the mainsheet led to a winch located on top of the coach-roof meaning by the time you move around the wheel and release the sheet from the winch the cockpit could be filling with water. Safely gybing (jibing in the USA) the mainsail with this sheet arrangement would not be easy.

Steering

Being stuck at the helm is the maritime version of wearing a ball and chain. It limits your ability to attend to other things that need to be done and can turn what would otherwise be a relaxing and enjoyable sail into a chore that is physically and mentally draining.

Figure 40 – a typical self-contained electric autopilot for a tiller steered yacht

Although some boats will sail a straight line on their own, particularly once you have adjusted the sail trim and maybe lashed the helm, they will not do this in all conditions. Some form of self-steering system is a great advantage. The wind-vane types have the benefit of needing no electrical energy, so you will have unlimited passage times.

However, the coastal sailor does not need to be so frugal with stored energy and may be better off with an electronic autopilot. There will be added complications or cost if your yacht is wheel steered rather than tiller.

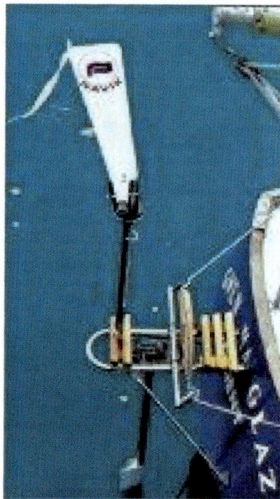

Figure 41 – a wind-vane steering system

Before engaging the electronic autopilot it is worth taking a few minutes to trim and balance the sails so the tiller (or wheel) is as neutral as possible so the autopilot has minimal work to do to hold a course. This ensures least use of your battery capacity.

Mooring alongside

Entering and leaving marinas, mooring to and departing from harbour quays, and going through locks are the most common fears that inhibit sailors from going it alone. These fears are understandable. These manoeuvres have to be performed in close proximity to hard structures and other boats where the opportunity for damage to your boat and your pride are high, not to mention damage to others' property.

You are at the mercy of unpredictable winds and currents that are being bent and disturbed by all those close structures. To make matters worse, you have no one else to blame if anything goes wrong and there is a good chance you will have an audience! All this can easily convince you that there is no way you will ever venture out alone but do consider that you are not the first person to do it. With good planning, preparation and practice, plus knowing what solutions will work and what will not in each situation, you will soon overcome your worries.

Mooring alongside involves a number of simultaneous tasks that are much better performed by a team of experienced people who are all aware of the plan, well briefed by the skipper, and have been delegated specific roles. Yet all this does not mean you cannot succeed on your own. If you pick your locations and weather conditions carefully, plan thoroughly and be brave, you can do it.

First, regarding location and weather conditions, as far as is possible make sure you do not start a manoeuvre in conditions beyond the capability of the single-hander. You need to know what you and your boat are capable of doing. If you are aiming for a berth at the far end of a marina and a force six is blowing from behind, the smartest plan may be to change your plan.

Don't assume that there are no alternatives and hope you get away with it, even if you are aiming for your regular berth. Far better to pick a more convenient position to moor where you can better cope with the strong wind or current, even if that means temporarily mooring alongside another boat or entering a berth marked 'private'. Once you are safely tied up and out of danger you can then seek advice (you may be told you can stay where you are!) or ask someone to help you move to the correct berth.

If the harbourmaster asks you to go to a berth you are not confident in entering, do tell him or her. These people understand and would rather not have an accident on their hands.

Another option in avoiding a difficult berth is to moor upwind or up current in another, easier, berth and then use ropes to controllably warp your boat into the intended one. For this situation you need to ensure you have one, preferably two, very long mooring warps, say, 20 or 30 metres long, made from polypropylene (i.e. a floating rope). Not Polyester /Dacron or Nylon. Do inform the harbourmaster before spanning fairways with ropes.

This warp can then be thrown or, with a small fender tied to the end, floated across the water and then used to gently pull your boat across to the other side. Choose the type of rope carefully, as some 3-strand polypropylene ropes in particular can be stiff and tangle easily. Braided or multi-plait polypropylene, like that used for water skiing tow-ropes are ideal They are designed to be non-tangle and at 8mm diameter are strong enough for warping most yachts although a little slender to grip.

Another good product is the Palm throw-bag: http://www.palmequipmenteurope.com/search/product-category/safety-and-rescue with a 20m long 10mm diameter floating line. Throw-bags are a very efficient way of passing a rope but do not be tempted by those with very light lines which you then use to haul a stronger line across. This takes twice as long and defeats the objective of a fast line transfer at which the throw-bag excels.

Figure 42 – a throw-bag and how to throw one using an under-arm action

Even if you have no helper to throw the line to, you can often throw it over a pontoon or onto the deck of another boat and then walk round and retrieve it. Likewise, a line floated across an expanse of water to another berth will often stay there, held by the wind and/or current until you can get there. You need to be patient and be prepared to spend some time to get everything in place before warping your boat across. Every situation will be different. The important thing is to take the time to think through a procedure until you are confident it will work.

While we are talking about long buoyant mooring warps, you should also invest in the largest fenders you can stow on board and have enough of them rigged along both sides of your boat. You cannot rely on the crew to swap sides at the last moment due to a change of plan, and big fenders can prevent a lot of damage.

Figure 43 – a mid-ships mooring cleat

The next vital piece of kit is a big strong mooring cleat fixed on both sides of your deck and just over half way along. Always a useful addition to any boat, these mid-ship cleats are invaluable to the single-hander and are seldom fitted by the boat builder. When coming alongside you should ideally have six mooring lines neatly coiled with the ends made fast to the bow, mid-ships and stern on both sides. Now, if there is no one ashore to catch your lines and you are not able to step ashore carrying two of them, at the very least you should be holding the mid-ships warp and the others will be ready to hand.

Making the mid-ships line fast to the nearest bollard will successfully restrain your craft from moving too far until you can get the other lines ashore and moor securely. If you are able to reach a dock-side bollard or cleat from the cockpit then, with a large loop in the end of the mid-ships mooring line, you can drop the loop over the bollard and motor gently forward with the tiller pushed over towards the dockside. With sufficient revs on the engine you will be able to hold your boat securely against the wall with the single line taking the strain while you fasten the rest of the shore-lines.

When entering a lock with a strong cross wind, do not be tempted to take the easy option and let your boat drift sideways to the downwind wall. That would be a good plan if you were going to stay there in the hope that the wind would have changed direction by the time you leave, but getting away from a wall or pontoon when pinned there by a cross-wind is not easy. If you do get into this situation and where it is possible, such as in a lock, the best way is to rig a bow and stern line to the other side by walking the lines around the lock and manually hauling your yacht across to the windward side and motoring off from there. Should you see a boat already moored to the windward side, hail the owner and moor alongside.

The standard advice on manoeuvring away from an alongside berth, particularly against a cross-wind, is to motor against a bow or stern spring. Once the other end of the boat has been coaxed far enough from the side, you cast off the spring, engage the other gear and motor off sharply. However, this is a very difficult procedure for the single-handed sailor as it can easily go wrong without at least one other person to help.

With no one ashore to release the spring, the usual method is to use a long loop of warp around the shore-cleat and lead back aboard. In this way you can release the end of the warp from the boat and haul the other end until the whole lot is safely back on deck. Doing this smoothly to avoid any snarl-ups and ensuring all the rope is out of the water and on board before going back to the cockpit and engaging the propeller takes time, usually longer than it takes for the wind to blow your boat back against the wall.

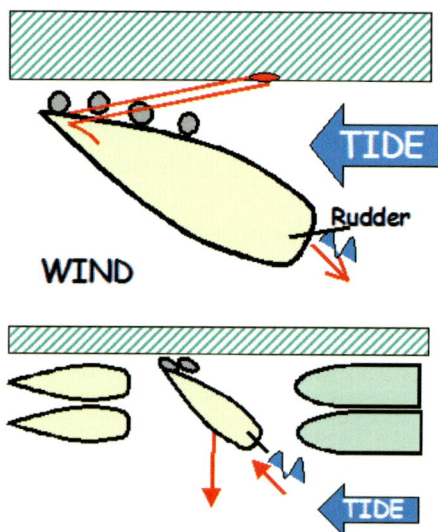

Figure 44 – manoeuvring away from a pontoon using a bow spring, very difficult alone

Springing the bow off is easier than the stern because you can usually do everything from the cockpit and if necessary you can just release the end of the warp, engage forward and motor off with the line trailing in the water behind you. Then you can retrieve the trailing line while still motoring forwards. This is risky, however, because if you have to unexpectedly slow down before you have retrieved the line it could end up around your propeller.

The best advice is not to get yourself into a position where you need to spring off, but life is never that simple or predictable. Here are some techniques for you to experiment with to increase your chances of success.

To save time and hopefully avoid possible snarl-ups when casting off and hauling aboard the spring, just unfasten it from your boat, leaving the shore end attached to the shore and let it drop into the water out of the way. A nylon or polyester rope that sinks is preferable. Once away, re-moor in a position that will not require a spring in order to leave again, and then walk back and retrieve your line.

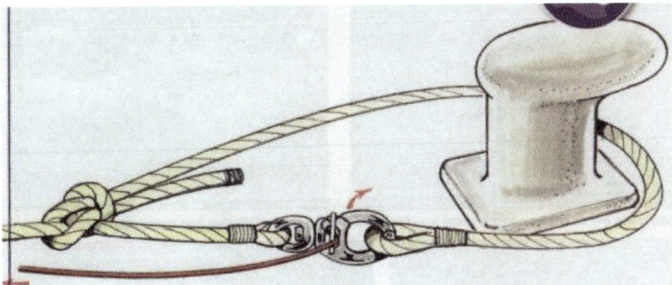

Figure 45 – a quick-release snap-shackle used in conjunction with a spring

Here is another method. Make yourself a dedicated springing line with a quick release snap-shackle on the end. A light line, running back alongside the main spring is pulled at the appropriate time to trigger the release on the snap-shackle, which then releases the loop that was round the shore-side bollard or cleat. With this method you only have half the length of spring to retrieve and minimal chance of getting it snagged in the process.

For this application you need the type of snap-shackle that has a trigger running parallel with the line, unlike the majority of those designed for yachts that have a trigger at 90-degrees. Those designed to release water-skiing tow-ropes in an emergency are good.

Figure 46 – quick-release snap-shackles for use on a spring line (left - Plastimo ref number 31452 150kg Safe Working Load) (right - Wichard WD-2575 1280kg SWL)

If you need to use a spring to get yourself out from between two other boats, one ahead and one astern of you, rather than the spring try to use the current if it is running down the line of boats. By pushing the appropriate end of your boat away from the pontoon and using the engine to hold your position, the current acting at an angle to the hull and keel will push you slowly sideways. This is probably, of course, the reverse procedure you had used to get yourself into that tight berth in the first place!

Remember, you can always use ropes to warp your boat alongside the boat ahead or astern of you, taking care to fend off as you do. Once alongside the other boat you will probably have more space to just motor off without the need for a spring line. Also, if alongside a beamy sail-boat you can position your boat to be nearer one end of the other boat so that, due to the curvature of the boats, yours will be at an angle to the quayside with the bow out and better positioned to motor off ahead.

Swinging moorings

There are many methods of picking up a swinging mooring. If it is your home mooring, you probably already have a solution that works well for you. However, when visiting another location you are often confronted with a range of facilities from a large metal eye on top of the floating buoy to a small pick-up buoy attached to the chain beneath the main buoy, and many other combinations.

The process of attaching your boat to the mooring is largely a single-handed job anyway. For you, the difference is that you will be both the grabber and the person driving the boat up to the mooring and, if you do not make the attachment quickly, will probably be hanging on desperately with no one to hand you another length of rope to take the strain. One solution is to always keep a spare length of line on the foredeck, coiled and securely fastened so it cannot get washed overboard. A 4m length of 10 or 12mm rope will suffice. You will not need it often but on those occasions when something goes wrong and you need a quick backup, that piece of line will be a life-saver.

Figure 47 – a well secured coil of rope stored on a foredeck for quick use in picking up a mooring

The first thing to do is to practice sailing or motoring up to a buoy in a range of different wind and current conditions with the objective of making your boat keep station, but with just a little forward way on, for as long it takes for you to walk to the bow and hook onto the mooring. In certain conditions you will find it better to leave the engine running in slow ahead while you go forward, in other conditions you will find it is not. It is critical that you learn what those conditions are.

It's worth experimenting by using the autopilot, if you have one, to help maintain direction. While you have just a little forward way through the water, especially if you are stemming a current, the autopilot should make a contribution.

To increase your chances of a first-time success, for mooring buoys with a metal ring or rope loop sticking out of the top, you could invest in one of the proprietary boathooks designed for the job. They fall into two basic types -- the ones that enable you to pass a line through the loop and the ones that attach the end of the line to the loop with a type of snap-hook. The latter can also be used to hook onto the line of a pick-up buoy.

Figure 48 –using a line to lasso a mooring buoy

A method that works on a wide variety of mooring types is a line, say 8m long, with both ends attached to the bow and using the loop produced to lasso the buoy. Just throw the loop so it falls around the mooring then as you pull on the rope it slides under the buoy and catches around the chain. However, this works only if the rope is sufficiently weighted so it sinks quickly. Even if using non-buoyant polyester or nylon rope it does not always sink in time before the strain comes on, and it can slip back over the top of the buoy. Half a metre length of 6mm chain inserted in the middle of the line to add weight works well and has the benefit of the chain offering better chafe resistance should you chose to hang on this pick-up line for any length of time.

Always add a second line to the mooring if staying longer or overnight as this lasso arrangement can slip back off over the buoy if the line goes slack when the tidal current changes direction. Slipping the mooring is also easy by just releasing one end from the boat and pulling the other back on board.

Anchoring

Dropping the anchor is an essential skill for any sailor, although many prefer to head for a swinging mooring and therefore never get enough practice at anchoring. If you are not already confident when sailing with crew, please do more to gain experience before you progress to solo sailing. When on your own it is more likely you will need to anchor as a way of stopping to sort out or fix something else; a good way of buying time.

Anchoring and weighing anchor under sail, without the use of the engine, is an even more difficult but useful and rewarding ability. However, the single-hander should preferably have the sails stowed and use the engine, if you have one. Using the motor to control your position is certainly easier and therefore safer in your situation. Save engine-less anchoring for a later date.

If you have a powered anchor capstan or windlass with the controls in the cockpit and an anchor that self-launches and stows, there will be no difference in your technique now that there is just you on board. Without this aid you need to take a little extra care.

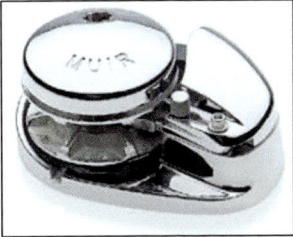

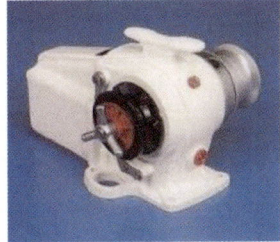

Figure 49 – a power capstan (left) and windlass (right) are a big help to the lone sailor

It is important that you increase the chances of the anchoring process working first time. With crew to help it is not such a chore to re-anchor but alone, at the end of a voyage when you are tired, you will quickly become exhausted if you have to retrieve all that heavy chain and do it all again. Applying that extra effort and sapping your energy can easily lead to a situation where things start to go wrong and you are then not in a condition to put right. The key, once again, is planning and preparation.

Before you arrive at the anchorage, check the chart and the height of tide and work out how much cable you will need. Then, flake this amount on the foredeck and cleat it. The cleating is the important step here. It means that if you need to get the anchor down quickly so as to get back to the cockpit to do something else, you will have one less job to tackle.

To increase the chance of the anchor digging in first time it is important that you do not let the anchor and chain run quickly over the bow roller all at once. This can easily lead to some of the chain falling on top of and getting caught on the anchor. You must lower the anchor steadily until the hook touches the bottom. Then, being sure the boat is making sternway in the current and/or wind, feed out the cable so it lies along the bottom until you have enough scope for the depth of water before the load comes onto the anchor. This provides the best chance of the anchor digging in first time.

If you cleat the cable with less scope out, hoping to dig it in before releasing the remainder of the cable, you may be disappointed. In this situation the chain or rope will not initially pull at the very low angle required for the anchor to work effectively, so it is more likely to skid over the surface until you are then not in the position of your choice. It is better to lay out too much, ensure the anchor bites effectively and then shorten the scope to reduce your swinging radius, than to start with too little cable.

It is possible to drop anchor from the cockpit by leading the cable from the bow, outside everything, back to the cockpit from where you can lower it over the side. Once the anchor bites, the boat will swing then ride by the bow. This is much easier to do with a rope cable, with the anchor and short length of chain in the cockpit and the rope leading round to the bow where the rest is flaked out ready to run. Then you do not have to contend with the weight of the chain leading around the gunwale trying to pull everything overboard before you are ready.

Yet, anchoring from the cockpit is not as simple as it may at first seem. It is far more difficult to ensure the cable gets laid out on the seabed before the load comes on, and there is a risk that the boat will turn and the cable get caught round the keel or propeller or rudder before you are laying comfortably by the bow.

The basic process of weighing anchor will be the same as if you had crew. The single-handed sailor, however, has a problem once the hook breaks out of the sea-bed. Until you get back to the cockpit the boat is not fully under control because it will be free to drift and turn at the mercy of the current and wind. If you have lots of space this is not a problem, but in a crowded anchorage or narrow river you will have to act quickly.

If you are stemming the current without much wind you may find that setting the autopilot will help to keep the boat pointing in the same direction for a short while or even longer if you also put the engine in slow ahead to help relieve the load on the cable as you haul it in. Even so, and especially if you do not have an autopilot, you need to have a quick method of fixing the anchor at the stem-head, or on deck, so it cannot fall back over the side before you regain control back in the cockpit.

Breaking out an anchor that refuses to budge without a windlass, capstan or additional arm muscles can be a frustrating task. Do not simply try to use ever-increasing body effort. The last thing you need in this situation is a strained back. Assuming you have the cable up-and-down, the first option is to make it fast and wait. Even small amounts of movement of the boat from wind, current or even the wash of a passing boat can work wonders. A rising tide will help too.

If you are using all chain a useful device is a chain-stopper, which is a quick and easy way of locking the chain during the process of lowering or weighing the anchor by hand. The stopper could be just a notch cut into a piece of stainless steel plate, but the type that has the notch cut into a hinged flap can also be used as a ratchet when raising the anchor.

You can gain significant advantage by adding an additional line to the cable using a rolling-hitch or, if you are on all chain, a chain-hook, and leading the line to a winch or a block and tackle. Do not be afraid to hail a passing yacht for assistance. Just tying another boat alongside while on a short scope may, after a few minutes, have added just enough additional pull to do the trick.

Figure 50 – a chain stopper

If the anchor has snagged on something there is nothing much the single-hander can do that would not be tried by the fully crewed yacht. The final option is, as always, to tie a fender to the end of the cable and cast it off so you can continue on your way and return later with additional help. If you are using an all chain cable, do ensure the bitter end has a length of rope attached that allows it to be cut from on deck in order to release the chain.

Many books on sailing recommend the use of a tripping line as a way of recovering an anchor that is difficult to break out or snagged. In my experience the tripping line causes far more problems when weighing anchor under normal circumstances than it can solve on the rare occasion when you cannot retrieve the anchor without one.

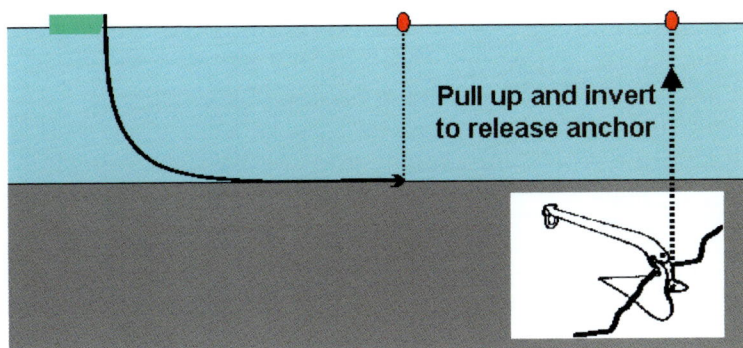

Pull up and invert to release anchor

Figure 51 – anchor tripping-line arrangement

The tripping line too easily can get caught round your propeller, jammed behind your rudder or snared by a passing boat. These things can happen when you are busy doing something else or during the actual process of weighing the anchor. Either way, you are going to have a big problem sorting out the mess with no one to help you.

As a single-hander, the last thing you want when anchoring is unnecessary complications. Do not rig a tripping line every time. Only when you have no other option than to anchor in a position where there is a risk of snagging something on the bottom (for example, in a river or harbour where there are swinging moorings nearby) should you consider rigging one.

When you must, then the best way to reduce the risk of problems is to have a line that is no more than two metres longer than the maximum depth in which you will be anchoring. A polyester or nylon line of 8mm diameter that does not float is best. Then, with one end tied to the anchor crown in the normal way, as you lower the cable tie the other end of the tripping line to the cable before feeding the remainder into the water. This way there is minimal line to get in a tangle. Once you have hauled in the cable and have it up-and-down, you will be able to retrieve the tripping line and use it to pull the fouled hook backwards, releasing it out of captivity.

Figure 52 – rowing out an anchor using the tender is not recommended when no one else is aboard the mother-ship

Rowing out an anchor using the tender after you have run aground is a standard procedure, enabling you to kedge the boat into deeper water once you are back aboard. But unless the conditions are ideal, this should not be attempted alone. Without the help of others too many things can go wrong and lead to a dangerous outcome. For example, what if the yacht's keel suddenly breaks free of the hump of mud on which it was stuck while you are still rowing with the anchor in the dinghy?

If you are lucky you may be able to toss the anchor over the side and hope it digs in while you row back to the mother-ship or you may be able to haul yourself back using the anchor cable. But both of these options have their inherent risks and are probably not worth trying when alone. Take a few moments to assess the risks before rushing into the tender, as it may be far safer to stay aboard, make yourself comfortable, and wait for the turn of the tide to re-float you.

Setting, reefing and stowing sails

You may think the answer is to have just one sail that can be raised, lowered or reefed just by pulling on one piece of rope. But if you want to go sailing in a range of wind strengths you will find that one sail is a poor compromise leading to an inefficient rig, sometimes needing lots of effort to operate and resulting in less enjoyment from your sailing.

In practice you will need two or more sails that you can hoist or reef, in different combinations, in order to cope with a reasonable variability in wind strengths and sea conditions. Do not assume this leads to excess complexity and is therefore beyond the ability of the average solo sailor. A gaff-cutter rig, for example, may have a complex array of lines but none of them needs much effort to operate since each of the sails is of modest area.

Having your sail area divided into two or more smaller sails also means you may not need to be reliant on mechanical winches to hoist them.

We do not always need to look back in time for solutions. The modern roller reefing and furling systems are a boon to the solo sailor. Yes, they are more prone to failure than a hanked-on jib, for example, but with a bit of basic maintenance they compensate significantly for the lack of crew. Roller systems are usually operated from the cockpit so setting, reefing and stowing sails become child's play.

A good compromise is to have roller reefing on the headsails and slab-reefing and lazy-jacks on the mainsail.

Lazy-jacks are an excellent, simple and affordable way of taming your mainsail.

Figure 53 – photograph of bungee-cord used as a captive sail-tie system

For stowing the mainsail, if you do not plan to use or fit a mainsail roller reefing or self-stacking system and instead rely on the traditional method of bunching the sail along the boom and tying it at intervals with sail-ties, you will have your hands full, literally. With only two hands and maybe just an autopilot in control of the helm, you need to tame and captivate the mainsail quickly so you can return to the cockpit.

Rather than loose sail-ties, try running two lengths of 8mm bungee cord the length of your boom either under or alongside it. At 1m intervals whip the pair together and, if possible, attach these junctions to the boom or the foot of the sail. In the middle of each 1m span, on one of the pair of cords only, you need a plastic hook. Now, to stow the mainsail, stretch the spans, one each side of and over the top of the sail, and hook them together. This process is very quick and the sail-ties are always in place ready for you.

There is very little chance of the hooks getting catapulted into your face with this arrangement, unlike what can happen when using individual bungee sail-ties. When the sail is raised the bungee cords just lay either side of the boom out of the way.

"Twenty years from now, you will be more disappointed by the things you did not do than by the things you did do. So, throw off the bowlines, sail away from the safe harbour. Catch the trade winds in your sails. Explore. Dream. Discover."

Samuel Langhorne Clemens, better known as "Mark Twain", who studied for his Mississippi steamboat pilot license in 1859.

Chapter 10

THE ESSENTIALS (LEGAL STUFF)

Do check that your insurance covers you for sailing alone. Some will not cover you and some will only cover you during daylight hours. Even if there is no exclusion shown in the policy document, you may have answered a relevant question about single-handing on the proposal form before you first took out the insurance. The proposal form you signed may have been completed many years ago before you had any intention of sailing alone and the insurance company can still refer to your declarations on that form when assessing a claim.

If you are in any doubt at all you should contact your insurer. As a result of negotiation, my current policy now has an additional condition which allows me to sail single-handed at night provided I have a working autopilot on board.

Vessels built or sold in the European Union since June 16, 1998, have to meet essential safety requirements as set out in the European Union Recreational Craft Directive (RCD) 2003/44/EC, which dictates specific categories of sea conditions for which the boat is designed. (See Chapter 1 for details.) Using your boat in sea conditions that it was not designed for may invalidate your insurance, not to mention the increased risk to which you are placing yourself.

Rule 5 of the International Regulations for Preventing Collision at Sea requires that a good lookout be kept at all times using eyes, ears, radar and VHF, particularly at night or in poor visibility. There is no concession for the single-handed sailor, so this puts the lone yachtsperson in a difficult situation.

SOLAS V for pleasure craft

Although not specifically aimed at the single-handed sailor, on July 1, 2002, some new international regulations came into force, which directly affect pleasure craft users. If something goes wrong, such as a collision (and, as mentioned in the previous section there is some doubt about the ability of the single-hander to keep a good lookout) then your case will look better if you can demonstrate your compliance with all other legalities.

These new regulations, https://www.gov.uk/government/publications/solas-regulations-for-pleasure-boat-users, are part of Chapter V of the International Convention for the Safety of Life at Sea, otherwise known as SOLAS V. Most of the SOLAS convention only applies to large commercial ships, but parts of Chapter V apply to small, privately owned pleasure craft.

The following requirements apply to all craft, irrespective of size. If you are involved in a boating accident and it is subsequently shown that you have not applied the basic principles outlined in this document, your insurance company may not look favourably on you, and in the extreme it may result in legal proceedings being taken against you.

VOYAGE PLANNING

Regulation V/34 -- *'Safe Navigation and avoidance of dangerous situations'* -- is a new regulation. It concerns prior-planning for your boating trip, more commonly known as voyage or passage planning. Voyage planning is basically common sense. As a pleasure boat user, you should particularly take into account the following points when planning a boating trip:

• **Weather:** Before you go boating, check the weather forecast and get regular updates if you are planning to be out for any length of time.

• **Tides:** Check the tidal predictions for your trip and ensure that they fit with what you are planning to do.

• **Limitations of the vessel:** Consider whether your boat is up to the proposed trip and that you have sufficient safety equipment and stores with you.

• **Crew** (in this case, you): Take into account the experience and physical ability of your crew. Crews suffering from cold, tiredness and seasickness won't be able to do their job properly and could even result in an overburdened skipper.

• **Navigational dangers:** Make sure you are familiar with any navigational dangers you may encounter during your boating trip. This generally means checking an up-to-date chart and a current pilot book or almanac.

• **Contingency plan:** Always have a contingency plan should anything go wrong. Before you go, consider bolt holes and places where you can take refuge should conditions deteriorate or if you suffer an incident or injury. Bear in mind that your GPS set is vulnerable and could fail at the most inconvenient time. It is sensible and good practice to make sure you are not over-reliant on your GPS set and that you can navigate yourself to safety without it should it fail you.

• **Information ashore:** Make sure someone ashore knows your plans and knows what to do should they become concerned for your well-being. The UK's Coastguard Voluntary Safety Identification Scheme (commonly known as CG66) is free and easy to join. The scheme aims to help the Coastguard to help you quickly should you get into trouble while boating. It could save your life.

RADAR REFLECTORS

Many large ships rely on radar for navigation and for spotting other vessels in their vicinity. So, whatever size your boat is, it's important to make sure you can be seen by radar. Regulation V/19 requires all small craft to fit a radar reflector "if practicable".

If your boat is more than 15m in length, you should be able to fit a radar reflector that meets the IMO requirements of 10m^2. If your boat is less than 15m in length, you should fit the largest radar reflector you can. Whatever the size of your boat, the radar reflector should be fitted according to the manufacturer's instructions, and placed as high as possible to maximise its effectiveness.

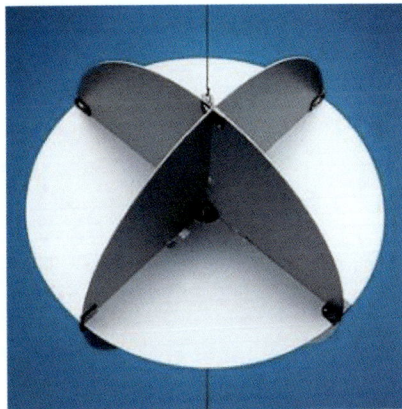

Figure 54 – typical radar reflectors

You may want to consider an active radar reflector, or transponder, that on detecting a radar beam sends back an amplified signal to ensure your small boat shows up on the other vessel's radar with a big image so it cannot be overlooked.

LIFE SAVING SIGNALS

Regulation V/29 requires you to have access to an illustrated document of the recognised life saving signals, so you can communicate with the search and rescue services or other boats if you get into trouble.

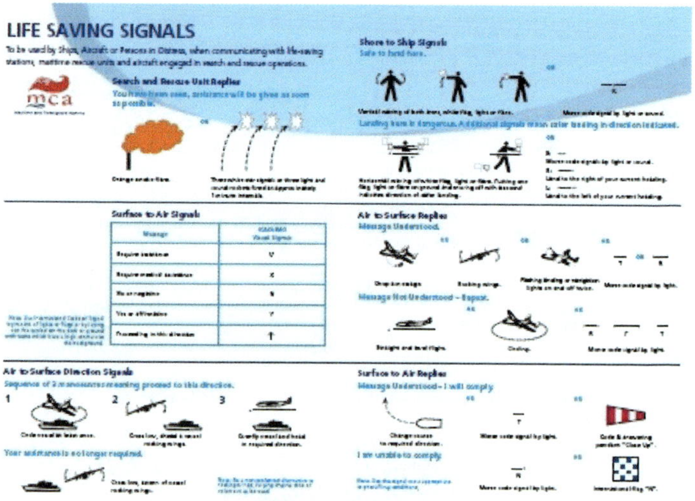

Figure 55 – SOLAS table of life-saving signals. You must have a copy of this on board

You can get a free copy of this table in a leaflet produced by the UK's MCA, available at https://mcanet.mcga.gov.uk/public/c4/solasv/mca%20docs/lifesaving%20sigs.pdf , or you can also find it in various nautical publications. If your boat, because it is small or very exposed, is not suitable for carrying a copy of the table on board, make sure you've studied the document before you go boating.

ASSISTANCE TO OTHER CRAFT
Regulations V/31, V/32 and V/33 require you to:

• Let the Coastguard and any other vessels in the vicinity know if you encounter anything that could cause a serious hazard to navigation, if it has not already been reported. You can do this by calling the Coastguard on VHF, if you have it on board, or by telephoning them at the earliest opportunity. The Coastguard will then warn other vessels in the area.

• Respond to any distress signal that you see or hear and help anyone or any boat in distress as best you can.

MISUSE OF DISTRESS SIGNALS
Regulation V/35 prohibits misuse of any distress signals. These are critical to safety at sea and by misusing them you could put your own or someone else's life at risk.

Chapter 11

READY TO CAST OFF!

Although you may now be more aware of the risks and of your limitations and vulnerabilities, most of what you do already when sailing with crew is exactly the same when without them. It is the very act of being aware that will make you a successful single-hander, so don't let what you have read above put you off sailing on your own.

Your very first passage alone will be a major step that you may have kept putting off for another day. Like all things in life, once you have some experience, and therefore confidence, you look back and wonder what all the fuss was about. Remember the first time you rode a bicycle, drove a car or cooked a meal for six?

There is no short term solution to gaining confidence. Experience produces confidence. Practice when you do have crew on board but ask them to let you do everything. They may be quite happy with that arrangement!

It may be easier to get started if you are using your existing boat, but if you are buying one specifically with single-handing in mind you will need to spend some time getting used to the boat and how it behaves with crew before venturing out alone.

Take it in small steps. Practice leaving, then immediately return to your home mooring. Progress in fine weather with a short passage and work up your experience.

You will find no formal training classes for single-handed sailing, so ask around the marina or yacht-club to make contact with other single-handers. Talk to them and ask one to go out sailing with you, or go sailing with them and see what they do.

In summary

The basics of sailing and navigating a sail boat are the same no matter how many crew are on board. The skipper just needs to share or delegate the tasks according to the number and ability of the available crew. But for you, the lone sailor with only one pair of hands, the secret is to be aware of your natural limitations, organise your boat, think ahead and plan so you are able to complete tasks in a logical and safe order.

The fact that you have just read this book means you are the type of person who researches and plans before taking action, so you already have some of the qualities of the single-handed sailor.

You are not the first. Many have gone before you. Just stand in any harbour or marina on a sunny summer's day and you will be sure to see a few coming or going. Our coasts are filled with sailors modestly sailing alone in all sorts of boats in all sorts of conditions. The vast majority never cross oceans or become famous or never write about it. They just get on with what they enjoy doing. And so should you. But prepare well, do it safely, and enjoy.

Just do it!

Happy solo coastal sailing.

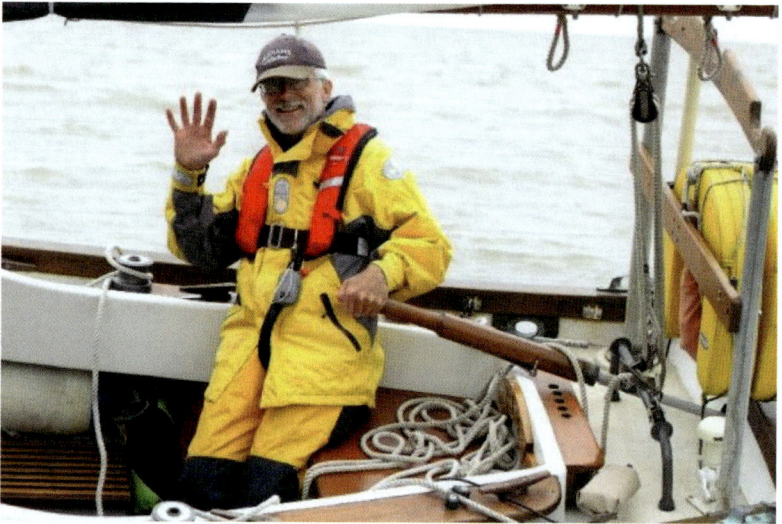
Photograph by Sue Feather

Appendix 1

List of Safety Equipment for Coastal Sailing

See also chapters 5 and 10. Obviously there is a limit to how much safety equipment you can carry if your boat is very small, but the following list is given as a guide. Even if you are intending to sail alone you should still consider being equipped for when you have crew on board. It is recommended that you also consult the Royal Yachting Association's Boat Safety Handbook 2nd Edition (Product Code: G103).

In some countries there are legal requirements for their citizens' boats to carry specified equipment. In most cases, when visiting another country it is accepted that you comply with the regulations of your own country and not the one you are visiting, but do please check what may apply to you.

Keeping out of, or recovering from, the water

- Lifejacket with combined harness for each person on board, with crotch strap(s), a whistle, a light, yacht name, and retro-reflective material. Also, a safety line, as short as is practical but not more than 2m long, with a double-action snap hook at each end.
- Lifebuoys for instant use with the yacht's name on them and fitted with retro-reflective material. One equipped with a whistle, a drogue, a self-igniting light and a pole and flag (a danbuoy). A second lifebuoy or a life-sling that can be trailed from a buoyant line at least 30m long.
- A buoyant throwing line or throw-bag, 15 to 25m long, readily accessible in cockpit.

- A boarding ladder or other boarding device, either fixed at the stern or capable of being deployed by a person in the water.
- Jackstays along port and starboard sides but as close to the centreline as possible and suitable points in the cockpit for clipping safety lines to.
- A life-raft with an in-date manufacturer's or approved agent's inspection certificate, of sufficient capacity to carry all the crew likely to be on board or an inflatable dinghy carried inflated or a rigid dinghy with adequate buoyancy and oars.

(OK so you may think some of the above is not relevant to single-handing but one day you may decide to take a crew or you may be able to pick up someone overboard from another boat)

Keeping the water out
- Two bilge pumps; one may be substituted with an electric pump, capable of operation with all hatches closed. Unless permanently fitted, bilge pump handles must be attached with a lanyard.
- Two buckets of not less than 9 litres capacity, fitted with a lanyard and a strong handle.
- A hand bailer for small boats.
- A seacock on all through-hull fittings that are below or close to the water.
- Softwood tapered plugs securely attached adjacent to each through-hull fitting so it can be blocked up.

Being seen, keeping a lookout and calling for help

- Navigation lights and foghorn to comply with the International Regulations for Preventing Collision at Sea for when sailing, motoring or at anchor.
- Day signal shapes i.e. motoring cone and anchor ball.
- Radar reflector permanently mounted, or capable of being hoisted to, at least 5m above deck with the largest practical RCS (radar cross-section), ideally at least 10m^2.
- A VHF marine radio transceiver with Digital Selective Calling (DSC) having an output power of 25W, audible from the helm, with a masthead antenna and a separate emergency antenna.
- A hand-held waterproof VHF marine radio transceiver plus an on-board battery charger and/or a pack of non-rechargeable batteries (which have a long shelf-life).
- A mobile phone in a waterproof bag (this should not be a substitute for marine VHF radio, just a back-up)
- Binoculars, preferably of 7X50 size.
- Water-resistant torch with spare bulb (unless an LED) and batteries, a head-mounted LED light and a high powered searchlight.
- An Automatic Identification System (AIS) if going anywhere near shipping channels.
- A radio receiver and a NAVTEX for weather forecasts.
- Distress flares, in-date, stowed in a watertight container:
  - 4 red parachute flares
  - 4 white hand held flares
  - 4 red hand held flares
  - 2 orange smoke
- A satellite Emergency Position Indicating Radio Beacon (EPIRB) registered with the appropriate authority and/or

a registered Personal Locator Beacon (PLB), with integral GPS, attached to each person.
- If based in the UK, boat and contact details submitted under the Coastguard Voluntary Safety Identification Scheme (commonly known as CG66).

Staying put, steering, towing and propulsion
- Two anchors each with a length of chain and warp, or chain only, suitable for the cruising area and size of boat.
- Towing warp, if no anchor warp is carried.
- Strong cleats or posts fore and aft for towing and being towed.
- Fenders and mooring warps plus some 20 to 30m warps.
- Emergency tiller or secondary steering device for wheel-steered yachts.
- Storm headsail and either a storm trysail or deep reef in the mainsail.
- Back-up propulsion (e.g. an outboard motor or a pair of oars or scull for smaller boats).
- A backup system for starting your engine (e.g. hand cranking or a second battery reserved for starting).

Fire-fighting and fuel safety
- When cooking or engine fuel is on board, one fire blanket and two multi-purpose extinguishers plus a fixed automatic or semi-automatic fire-fighting system in the engine-compartment. Put an extinguisher on either side of the stove in case you are on the "wrong side" when a fire starts.
- Audible gas and carbon monoxide detectors.
- All gas and spare/reserve petrol to be stored in appropriate vented lockers with overboard drains.

Navigational equipment

- Up-to-date paper charts together with tide tables and other navigational publications.
- The means to plot a position onto a paper chart (e.g. parallel rule, dividers, pencil, etc.).
- A means of fixing a position at all times (e.g. GPS receiver or chart plotter).
- Steering and hand-bearing compasses that can be read in the dark.
- Echo-sounder plus a lead-line for backup.
- A system for measuring speed through the water and/or over the ground.
- A watch or clock.
- A light, preferable a red one which will not affect your night-vision too much, to see charts, etc.

Personal safety and first-aid

- A first-aid kit and instruction manual.
- Protection from the sun, the wet and the cold and a spare set of dry clothes.
- Spare spectacles.
- It is highly recommended that each person on board carries a knife at all times whilst at sea.
- A mobile telephone/cell-phone to keep those ashore informed of your whereabouts, plus a spare battery or a method of charging the battery while on-board.

Tools & spares

- Toolkit suitable for general, rig, engine and electrical repairs.
- Spare shackles, rope, pulley blocks, split-pins, self-adhesive sailcloth, fuses, bulbs, hose, hose clips, stove lighter, fuel, batteries, electrical wire, oil, grease, filters,

drive-belts, pump impellers, water, self-amalgamating tape, etc.

Appendix 2

Sources of Further Information

Although most of the links below are not specific to single-handed coastal sailing, they are particularly recommended.

- A good yacht safety website produced by the UK's Royal National Lifeboat Institution (RNLI) http://completeguide.rnli.org/

- The UK's Royal National Lifeboat Institution (RNLI) site can be found at www.rnli.org.uk . This organisation provides a lifeboat service around the UK and Republic of Ireland and is funded solely from voluntary contributions.

- To join the UK's HM Coastguard's CG66 Voluntary Safety Identification Scheme go to https://mcanet.mcga.gov.uk/public/cg66

- The UK's Maritime and Coastguard Agency (MCA) is the Government funded organisation committed to preventing loss of life, continuously improving maritime safety, and protecting the marine environment: https://www.gov.uk/government/organisations/maritime-and-coastguard-agency

- Information on boat safety from the United States of America's Coast Guard at http://www.uscgboating.org/

- Details of the Global Maritime Distress and Safety System (GMDSS) can be found here http://www.icselectronics.co.uk/support/info/gmdss

- To register an Emergency Position Indicating Radio Beacon (EPIRB) or Personal Location Beacon (PLB) in the UK go to https://forms.dft.gov.uk/mca-sar-epirb/

- To look up a station's VHF radio MMSI number go to http://www.itu.int/cgi-bin/htsh/mars/ship_search.sh

- The UK's Royal Yachting Association (RYA), founded in 1875, is the UK's premier membership organisation for recreational boat owners and crew http://www.rya.org.uk

- Information about cruising in dinghies can be found at the Dinghy Cruising Association http://dinghycruising.org.uk/

- The Old Gaffers Association, a favourite of mine, aims to preserve interest in and encourage development of Gaff Rig, and to participate in the maintenance of our Maritime Heritage.
  UK site: http://www.oga.org.uk/
  Fench site:- http://www.old-gaffers.com/
  In the Netherlands http://www.oldgaffers.nl/
  In Australia:- http://www.gaffrigsailinginwa.org/

A rewarding end to a successful passage.

The End

About me

My 45-plus years of sailing experience include motor-boating, rowing, windsurfing and kayaking, as well a range of sailing boats. Currently I have three boats:

photograph by Tony Pickering

The Heard-23 Falmouth Working Boat "Plum" built by Martin Heard. She is lovely to sail and very stable. Although only just over 23 feet length on deck, length overall including the bowsprit is 35 feet!

The 11foot Coot design sailing dingy "Dabchick" designed by Andrew Wolstenholme, and built by me. She is such a pleasure to sail and is so easy to launch and recover from the slipway.

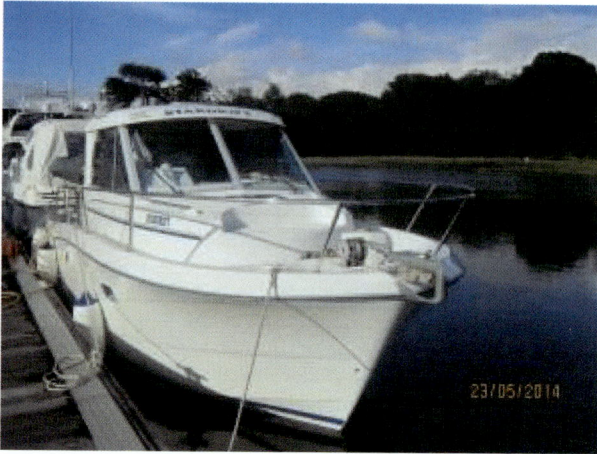

The Beneteau Antares 760 "Stardrift". Brilliant accommodation and sea-keeping for a boat only 26feet (8m) long.

You will see from the above I believe in diversity of boating.

Recently I have been doing some coxing in rowing gigs both for the South Woodham Ferrers rowing club and with the local Coastguard rowing team.

When not playing with boats I work for the UK Coastguard as a member of the South Woodham Coastguard Rescue Team. Alongside the other 340 teams in the UK we cover 70 miles of our local coastline and provide a 24/7 search and rescue resource, in conjunction with the Royal National Lifeboat Institution and other rescue services, with detailed local knowledge of the waters and coastline. (search on Facebook.com for "South Woodham Coastguard").

Somehow, in my spare time, I manage to be an Environmental Management Consultant, but that is another story......

29849198R00074

Printed in Great Britain
by Amazon